hm SCIENCE LEARNING AND STUDY SKILLS PROGRAM:

People, Energy, and Appropriate Technology

Revised Edition

Developed by The Study Skills Group

Authors: Carol Wilson
Wilson Educational Services

Gary Krasnow, *former Director*
Renewable Energy Resource Center
Connecticut Audubon Society

Editor: Lisa Smulyan

Senior Editor: David Marshak

Editorial Board: Kiyo Morimoto
Jerome Pieh

NSTA

National Science Teachers Association
Washington, DC 20009

nassp

The National Association of Secondary School Principals
Reston, Virginia 22091

Graphs on pages 42-47 adapted from *Annual Energy Review.* Washington, D.C.: Executive Office of the President, 1990.

Illustrator: Linda Sokol

Our thanks to all of the hundreds of teachers and students who used the first edition of the **hm Science Study Skills Program** and contributed their suggestions to us.

Our deep gratitude to two talented teachers who served as revision consultants for this new edition: Mary Gosse and Al Koehler.

Published in the United States of America
by Rowman & Littlefield Education
A Division of Rowman & Littlefield Publishers, Inc.
A wholly owned subsidiary of The Rowman & Littlefield Publishing Group, Inc.
4501 Forbes Boulevard, Suite 200, Lanham, Maryland 20706
www.rowmaneducation.com

ISBN 978-0-8108-3808-6

PO Box 317
Oxford
OX2 9RU, UK

NASSP
1904 Association Drive
Reston, VA 22901-1537
(703) 860-0200

Timothy J. Dyer, Executive Director
Thomas F. Koerner, Deputy Executive Director,
    Director of Publications
Patricia George, Project Manager

Copyright 1993 by NATIONAL ASSOCIATION OF SECONDARY SCHOOL PRINCIPALS. All rights reserved. Manufactured in the United States of America. All hm Learning and Study Skills materials are copyrighted. No portion of this publication or its accompanying materials may be reproduced or copied or stored in any information retrieval system without the written permission of NASSP.

TABLE OF CONTENTS

Introduction 1

Part One: What Makes A Technology Appropriate?

I.   Listening As A Science Skill *and* What Does Appropriate Mean? 2

II.   Building Your Science Vocabulary *and* What Makes A Technology Appropriate? 8

III.   Reading For Meaning *and* Domestic Petroleum: How Long Will It Last? 15

IV.   Taking Effective Notes *and* Sun, Wind, And Water: Hope For The Future? 23

V.   Making Judgments *and* How Does Technology Affect The Environment? 32

VI.   Working With Graphs *and* How Can We Use Energy Efficiently? 37

VII. Solving Problems *and* How Much Do Technologies Cost? 49

VIII. Becoming A Skilled Test Taker *and* Appropriate Technology In Review 60

Part Two: The Solar Greenhouse As An Appropriate Technology

IX.   Using Scientific Measuring Tools *and* Trapping The Sun's Energy 66

X.   Applying Scientific Laws *and* How Does Energy Behave In A Solar Greenhouse? 76

XI.   Working With The Metric System *and* How Can We Store Energy? 89

XII. Working With Large Numbers *and* How Can We Conserve Energy? 97

Part Three: Appropriate Technology At Work

XIII. Developing And Testing An Hypothesis *and* Applying Appropriate Technology 105

XIV. Putting It All Together 112

Glossary 118

PART ONE:

WHAT MAKES A TECHNOLOGY APPROPRIATE?

INTRODUCTION

WHAT ARE LEARNING AND STUDY SKILLS?

Learning and study skills are ways or methods of learning. Knowing a variety of learning and study skills and how to use them can help you become a more effective learner.

When you've developed learning and study skills, you will be able to make better use of your time and effort. You'll become a more independent learner and problem solver. An independent learner knows which questions to ask and how to find the answers to those questions.

LEARNING AND STUDY SKILLS IN SCIENCE

Some learning and study skills are useful in all subjects. Knowing how to listen, for example, will help you learn in any class. Other skills are most useful in a particular class or subject.

When you learn science learning and study skills, you find out how to learn science more effectively. For example, you discover how to read graphs and charts, how to take notes from your science textbook, how to work with large numbers and the metric system, and how to solve problems.

People develop learning and study skills best when they practice them. Each unit in this book will help you learn about useful learning and study skills and will give you a chance to practice those skills.

PEOPLE, ENERGY, AND APPROPRIATE TECHNOLOGY

As you practice science learning and study skills in this book, you will also have the chance to learn about some key ideas in science. As you examine the connections among people, energy, and technology, think about these questions:

Where does energy come from, and how is it used?
What makes one technology better, or more appropriate, than another?
How can people make the best use of the energy and technology available to them?

By the time you finish this book, you should be able to answer these questions and more about people, energy, and appropriate technology.

UNIT I: LISTENING AS A SCIENCE SKILL
and
WHAT DOES APPROPRIATE MEAN?

WHAT IS LISTENING?

What is *listening?* And what is the difference between listening and hearing?

You probably spend a lot of your time listening. In fact, students are asked to listen about 55% of the time that they are in school.

Think for a few moments about what you actually do when someone asks you to listen. Then define *hearing* and *listening* on the lines below.

hearing = _____

_____

listening = _____

_____

LISTENING IS A SKILL

Hearing takes place in your ears. It is a physical process. But listening is more than just hearing. Listening means paying attention to what you are hearing and trying to make sense of it.

People are not born as good listeners, but they can learn how to listen. Listening is a learning skill that you can learn through practice.

A good listener is an active listener. An active listener hears words as they are spoken and thinks about what they mean.

ACTIVE LISTENING

Active listening means *concentrating* and *participating*.

When you concentrate, you choose to direct your attention to what you are hearing. When you start to listen, tell yourself with your inner voice, "I am going to listen very carefully." Whenever you find that you are not listening, direct your attention again by repeating these words to yourself.

An active listener participates in what she or he is hearing. *Participating* means hearing the words that are spoken, thinking about what the speaker is saying, and trying to make sense of it.

Three ways to participate in what you are hearing are:

1. When you listen, ask yourself questions about what you are hearing. If you can, answer the questions.

2. Try to connect what you are hearing with what you already know.

3. Try to "picture" in your mind what is being said. Sometimes a picture can help you understand what the speaker is saying.

EXERCISE I

Directions: Your teacher will read a paragraph aloud to you. Listen carefully, using the three ways of participating in what you hear suggested above. Try to find the main idea of the paragraph. Write the main idea on the lines below.

Main idea: _____

_____

_____

_____

EXERCISE II

Directions: You will hear three different paragraphs about the same topic. Listen carefully, and try to find the theme or main idea common to all three paragraphs.

When you have heard all three paragraphs, work with your group to describe the theme or main idea shared by the three paragraphs. Then write the theme on the lines below.

You may want to jot down key words as you listen to help you remember. Use the space at the bottom of the page.

Theme/main idea: _____

_____

_____

_____

Key words:

TAKING NOTES

Taking notes is another way of becoming an active listener. To take useful notes, you need to pay attention to what you are hearing and think about what is worth writing down. When you take notes, you also create a record of what you have heard that you can use later.

One way to take notes is to write down *key words*. The steps for taking notes in this way are listed below:

1. Do not try to write down everything that you hear. Instead, listen for words that seem key or important, and jot these down. The speaker may define a key word, emphasize it, repeat it, give examples of it, or tell you in some other way to pay attention to it.

2. As you listen to a speaker, jot down all the key words that you hear. *Remember:* key words can be a single word or a group of words.

3. When the speaker is finished, go back to each key word and write something about it. Define it, use it in a sentence, and/or give examples of it. When you write about the key words, you make sure that you really understand what they mean.

EXERCISE III

Directions: Your teacher will read a passage to you. Listen carefully, and take notes by jotting down key words on the lines below.

When your teacher is finished, write what is important about each key word. Then describe the main idea of the passage in the space provided below.

Key words: _____

_____

_____

_____

_____

_____

_____

Main idea: _____

_____

_____

EXERCISE IV

Directions   Imagine that your science class is planning a day trip to the beach to examine the plants and animals that live there. In the space provided below, write three things it would be appropriate for you to bring, and three things that would be inappropriate for you to bring. On the line next to each object, explain why the object is appropriate or inappropriate for this trip.

Appropriate objects   **Why they are appropriate**

1. _____   _____

2. _____   _____

3. _____   _____

Inappropriate objects   **Why they are inappropriate**

4. _____   _____

5. _____   _____

6. _____   _____

UNIT I SUMMARY

LISTENING AND TAKING NOTES

Listening is a learning skill that involves paying attention to what you are hearing and trying to make sense of it.

A good listener is an *active listener*. Active listening means *concentrating* and *participating*.

Concentrating is choosing to direct your attention to what you are hearing, and choosing to keep listening if your attention wanders.

Participating is thinking about what the speaker is saying. To participate:

1. Ask yourself questions about what you are hearing, and answer them if you can.

2. Try to connect what you are hearing with what you already know.

3. Try to "picture" in your mind what is being said.

Taking notes is another way of listening actively. One way to take notes is to jot down key words in these ways:

1. Listen for words that seem important or key, and jot them down.

2. When the speaker is finished, go back to each key word and define it, use it in a sentence, or give an example of it.

WHAT DOES APPROPRIATE MEAN?

Anything that is appropriate fits the situation in which you use it. To see if something is appropriate, ask yourself:

Does it do the job and/or fit the situation?
Does it do too little or too much?
Is there anything that fits the situation better?

If it fits the job well, not by too little or too much, and if there is nothing that fits the situation better, then it is appropriate.

UNIT II: BUILDING YOUR SCIENCE VOCABULARY
and
WHAT MAKES A TECHNOLOGY APPROPRIATE?

INTRODUCTION

In your reading you will often come across words that you don't know.

Read the paragraph below. Then try to define each of the underlined words in the space provided beneath the paragraph. You're not expected to know all of the words. Just do the best you can!

> The concepts of environment and <u>ecosystem</u> have been around for a long time. But only in recent years have these ideas become familiar to most people. People have begun to realize that all living things depend on the ecosystem to which they belong. For living things to <u>sustain</u> themselves, they require a healthy environment.

ecosystem _____

sustain _____

LEARNING NEW WORDS

You may not have known the exact meanings of the words underlined in the paragraph above. Yet you were probably able to figure out a meaning for each word that helped you make sense of the paragraph.

Science has its own vocabulary or set of words. To understand what is going on in science, you need to know what the words mean. In this unit, you will learn two ways to find out the meanings of new words.

CONTEXT CLUES

You may have figured out the meaning of a new word in the paragraph above by thinking about the words and sentences around it. This is called getting the meaning from CONTEXT CLUES.

A CONTEXT is the setting in which something is found. For example, a jewelry store is a context in which rings are sold. A circus is a context where you would expect to find clowns and trapezes.

When you read, the CONTEXT is the words and sentences around a particular word. These familiar words and sentences, called CONTEXT CLUES, can often help you figure out the meaning of a word you do not recognize.

Example   Some sources of energy we now use will not last forever. For example, because the amount of oil left in the ground is <u>finite</u>, we have to find other sources of energy before it runs out.

finite means: _____

_____

EXERCISE I

Directions: Your teacher will read the passage below to you. As you read along, think about the meanings of the underlined words. When your teacher has finished reading, go back and underline the context clues that will help you define each underlined word. Then write a definition for each underlined word on the lines following the passage.

APPROPRIATE TECHNOLOGY

Michael and Maria Lopez used to grow their own vegetables every summer when they lived in a rural area. Then they moved into a second floor apartment on a busy street near downtown Boston, Massachusetts. No more pleasant afternoons caring for the garden. No more freshly picked vegetables for dinner every night. And no more savings on groceries at the market. Or so they thought, until they heard about a group of people who had formed an organization called Boston Urban Gardeners, or BUG.

With BUG's help, Michael and Maria joined a community garden project located in an empty lot just five blocks from their apartment. They were assigned a ten foot square plot of land to grow whatever they wished. Following the advice of more experienced members of BUG, they first revitalized the worn out earth by adding a layer of topsoil. The topsoil came from the BUG compost pile, which had been made from kitchen scraps, lawn cuttings, and leaves normally hauled away to the landfill. By showing their BUG membership card at local hardware and garden stores, they were able to save ten percent on many of their gardening supplies. Almost before they knew it, their seeds had sprouted. Within a matter of weeks they were once again enjoying freshly picked salads.

rural _____

urban _____

revitalized _____

compost _____

sprouted _____

EXERCISE II

Directions: The rest of the story about Maria and Michael Lopez uses the idea of appropriateness discussed in Unit I.

Read the rest of the story on the next page. When you find a word that stops you because you are not sure of its meaning, underline the word and write it on the lines below the story. Use context clues to figure out the meaning of the word you have written. Write your meaning in the space to the right of each word.

When you can't figure out the exact meaning of a word from the context clues, write down the best meaning you can, given the clues that you have.

APPROPRIATE TECHNOLOGY *(continued)*

Like Michael and Maria Lopez, we all need food on a daily basis in order to remain strong and healthy. Most of us depend on a network of people and services spread out all across the country to keep us from going hungry. For example, acres of wheat are grown by farmers in the Midwest, and then harvested, transported, milled into flour, and transported again, finally to appear as bread on your table. Many of the fruits and vegetables you enjoy are grown in the other states and shipped to you in refrigerated trucks.

In the recent years this nationwide food supply network has become more vulnerable and expensive. Insects, lack of rain, strikes by farm workers and truckers, problems with highways, and at times even energy shortages have all contributed to temporary food shortages and higher prices at the market. Winter storms, floods, and earthquakes could have an even more damaging effect in the future. Clearly, we need a more reliable system for feeding the nation. We can use appropriate technology to help find better ways to meet this basic human need.

Boston Urban Gardeners (BUG) is an example of people using appropriate technology to meet their own basic need for food. By using vacant lots from all over the city, making and using compost piles, and calling on the talents and enthusiasm of its members as well as other local resources, BUG has given people control over the production of their own summer vegetables.

Underlined words   **Definitions**

_____   _____

_____   _____

_____   _____

_____   _____

_____   _____

A FOOD NETWORK

LEARNING NEW WORDS: USING THE GLOSSARY

Sometimes you may not be able to find enough context clues to help you define a word you do not know. Or you may need to know the exact meaning of a word in order to understand the sentence or paragraph in which it appears. Science textbooks often have a small dictionary of new words at the end, called a GLOSSARY, which defines some of these words for you.

A GLOSSARY does not give you as much information about a word as a dictionary would, but it will give you the exact meaning of a word as your science book uses it. Using the GLOSSARY is a convenient way to learn new words as you read.

EXERCISE III

Directions: Below is a list of words from the "Appropriate Technology" story. Find each word in the Glossary on page 118. Write the definition given for each word on the line next to it.

Then, below each word, write a sentence in which you use the new word. In your sentences, try to include context clues that would help another person define the word.

Example   daily   every day

Sentence: Ann weeded the garden daily, because every day there were new weeds growing among the vegetables.

1. appropriate technology _____

   Sentence: _____

2. local _____

   Sentence: _____

(Continued on page 12)

3. resources _____

_____

Sentence: _____

_____

_____

4. disposal _____

_____

Sentence: _____

_____

_____

5. crisis _____

_____

Sentence: _____

_____

_____

EXERCISE IV

Directions: Below is a list of resources you use at home. We can get and dispose of these resources using technologies that are appropriate or inappropriate.

To the left of this list are spaces where you can check off where the resource comes from. To the right of the list, you can check off where you dispose, or get rid of, each resource.

Complete as much of this chart as you can, checking off where each resource comes from and how you dispose of it. You may need to ask your parents for help. You can also check package labels to find out where a resource comes from.

Do the best you can. If you do not use one of the resources listed in your home, or can't find out about where it comes from or how you dispose of it, leave that part of the chart blank.

HOME RESOURCE USE CHECKLIST

WHERE RESOURCE IS PRODUCED					WHERE YOU DISPOSE OF RESOURCE			
Locally	In Your State	In United States	In Another Country	RESOURCE USED AT HOME	Landfill	Sewer	Burn	Recycle
				Eggs				
				Meat				
				Bread				
				Dairy Products				
				Fruits/vegetables				
				Plastic bottles				
				Glass bottles				
				Aluminum cans				
				Newspaper				
				Fertilizer				
				Water				
				Electricity				
				Gasoline				
				Oil				
				Coal				
				Natural gas/propane				
				Solar energy				

UNIT II SUMMARY

LEARNING NEW WORDS IN SCIENCE

You will often come across new words when reading your science materials. Two ways of finding out what these words mean are using *context clues* and using the *glossary* of terms in your science book.

Context clues are familiar words and phrases in a sentence or paragraph. From these words, you can often figure out the meaning of an unknown word.

The *glossary* is a small dictionary in your science book. It provides you with the exact meaning of the word as it is used in your book.

APPROPRIATE TECHNOLOGY

Technologies are the methods, systems, tools, and machines we use to accomplish a task.

Appropriate technologies:

- use local talents and resources,
- can be understood, created, operated, and repaired by the people who depend on them,
- are usually smaller and less expensive than more complicated technologies.

Communities can use appropriate technologies to solve their own problems and meet their basic needs.

UNIT III: READING FOR MEANING
and
DOMESTIC PETROLEUM: HOW LONG WILL IT LAST?

INTRODUCTION

Your science teacher often asks you to read through a chapter or some other materials on your own. A good way to start is to SURVEY the reading.

To SURVEY a reading
- look at the *title* of the reading,
- look at the *headings* and *subheadings* throughout the reading, which are usually in darker or larger print than the rest of the reading, and
- read the *introduction* and *conclusion* or summary, or the first and last paragraphs of the reading. If you are surveying a paragraph, read the first and last sentences.

By SURVEYING a reading before you read it, you can usually find out what it is about and what its main points are. Surveying prepares your mind to take in the details presented in the main text of the reading.

EXERCISE I

Directions: Your teacher will give you 2-3 minutes to *survey* this unit, "Reading for Meaning," using the steps listed above.

After you have surveyed this unit, use the space below to write three things you expect to learn from reading the unit.

I EXPECT TO LEARN:

1. _____
   _____
   _____

2. _____
   _____
   _____

3. _____
   _____
   _____

READING FOR MEANING: FOUR STEPS

One way of becoming a more effective reader of science books and articles is to use a set of four steps that help you find the most important points in the reading. You have already practiced the first step, SURVEYING, in the Introduction to this unit and in Exercise I.

The four steps of reading for meaning that you will learn in this chapter are:
- SURVEY
- READ
- MAP
- CHECK

READING: MAIN IDEAS AND SUPPORTING DETAILS

Once you have surveyed a reading, the second step in reading for meaning is to READ. As you read, you need to identify the *main ideas* and *supporting details* of each paragraph or section.

> The MAIN IDEA is the most important idea of the paragraph or section. The rest of the paragraph or section is built around this central idea. The main idea is often, but not always, contained in the first sentence of the paragraph or section.

> SUPPORTING DETAILS explain, prove, or tell something about the main idea of the paragraph or section. They make the main idea clearer or give more information about it.

Identifying main ideas and supporting details as you read will help you remember the important information in your science reading.

Example: Find the main idea and supporting details in this paragraph:

> Boston Urban Gardeners (BUG) is an example of people using appropriate technology to meet their own basic need for food. By using vacant lots from all over the city, making and using compost piles, and calling on the talents and enthusiasm of its members as well as other local resources, BUG has given people control over the production of their own summer vegetables.

Main idea: _____

_____

Supporting details: _____

_____

_____

_____

EXERCISE II

Directions: Survey and then read the passage "Spaceship Earth" given on the next page. In the space provided, write the main idea of each paragraph and list the details that support that main idea.

SPACESHIP EARTH

When a spaceship blasts off it must carry all the fuel it needs for its entire voyage. But the amount of fuel it can carry is limited. Like a spaceship, the planet Earth has a limited amount of fuel available for use.

Over 90% of the energy used in the U.S. today comes from finite sources within the earth, such as coal, natural gas, and petroleum. To make matters worse, we are using them up faster than new deposits can form. For example, it takes more than one million years for decaying plants and animals to become petroleum. In the last one hundred years, we have used more than half of the known world supply of petroleum. No one knows for sure when we will run out of non-renewable sources of energy, such as coal, oil, and natural gas, but some people predict that it may happen within your lifetime.

Paragraph 1

Main idea: _____

_____

Supporting details: _____

_____

_____

_____

Paragraph 2

Main idea: _____

_____

Supporting details: _____

_____

_____

"Be sure we have enough ... we don't want to run out between here and Mars."

MAPPING

The third step in reading for meaning in science is taking notes. Taking notes helps you to keep track of the main ideas and supporting details you identify as you read.

MAPPING is one way to take notes about what you read. To make a map of your reading:

- Find the main idea. Write it down and circle it.
- As you identify supporting details, write them on lines connected to your main idea circle.

Your map will look something like this:

supporting detail — (MAIN IDEA) — supporting detail

When you are done, your map will remind you of the most important points in your reading.

Example: Below is one student's map of the second paragraph of "Spaceship Earth."

- takes more than 1 million years to form oil
- such as coal, oil, natural gas
- (U.S. energy comes from non-renewable sources)
- may be all gone in our lifetime
- used up faster than it is replaced

EXERCISE III

Directions: Read the first two paragraphs of "The U. S. Oil Supply: 1973 and Today" below. In the space provided, make one map that shows the main idea and supporting details included in these two paragraphs.

THE U. S. OIL SUPPLY: 1973 and Today

An energy crisis occurred in 1973 when the Organization of Petroleum Exporting Countries (OPEC) announced it would no longer sell oil to the United States. This situation only lasted for a few months, but that was long enough to make Americans aware of how much they depended on the countries in OPEC for gasoline and heating oil.

As a result of this crisis, energy experts in the U.S. came up with a plan to reduce our need to import oil from other countries. The experts said that if we conserved oil and looked for more petroleum in our own country, we could supply most of our own by the year 2000. It seemed like a good plan at the time, but we now know that it won't work.

MAP:

CHECKING

When you have surveyed, read, and mapped a reading, the final step is to CHECK what you have learned. CHECKING helps you remember the most important points in the reading.

You can CHECK yourself in the following ways:

1) Ask yourself, "What is the most important idea(s) I have learned from this reading?"

2) Discuss the reading with other people who have read it.

EXERCISE IV

Directions: Re-read the first two paragraphs of "The U. S. Oil Supply: 1973 and Today" on page 19. Then read the next three paragraphs below. In the space provided on the next page, 1) *map* the last three paragraphs, and 2) *check* yourself on what you have learned by writing two or three sentences that explain the most important ideas from "The U. S. Oil Supply: 1973 and Today."

THE U. S. OIL SUPPLY: 1973 and Today (continued)

The United States now depends both on domestic and foreign oil. Domestic production is the oil that we pump from wells in our own country. In 1980 we pumped 3.14 billion barrels of domestic petroleum out of the ground. In 1985 we pumped 3.25 billion barrels, and in 1990 we removed another 2.78 billion barrels. According to U.S. government figures, our proven reserves, or the amount of petroleum left in the ground that can be sold at a profit, had shrunk to only 25.9 billion barrels by 1991.

If we continue to pump almost 3 billion barrels of our own petroleum each year without increasing our proven reserves, they will be gone within ten years. Of course, the discovery of new petroleum in the U.S. goes on. These new reserves are added to our proven reserves, making it unlikely that we will actually run out of petroleum in this ten year period.

Yet the supply of domestic petroleum, a non-renewable resource, is limited. Many people believe that the U.S. will run out of petroleum within the next several decades. At that point we will either have to depend on other countries for oil or substitute other forms of energy.

1. MAP of these three paragraphs:

2. CHECK on "The U. S. Oil Supply: 1973 and Today": _____

_____

_____

_____

_____

UNIT III SUMMARY

READING FOR MEANING

The four step method of reading for meaning will help you learn and remember more from your science readings. All four steps ask you to think about the *main ideas,* or most important points, in the reading, and the *supporting details* that back up those points.

To read for meaning:

- SURVEY: Look quickly over the titles, introduction, headings, and conclusion, or first and last paragraphs or sentences. Surveying tells you what the main ideas of a reading are.

- READ: As you read, focus on the main ideas and supporting details.

- MAP: Make a map that shows the main ideas and supporting details. A map helps you keep track of important information as you read. It also gives you notes you can use later.

- CHECK: Look over your mapped notes and remind yourself what this reading is about. Ask yourself, "What have I learned from this reading?"

NON-RENEWABLE ENERGY

Most of the energy we use today comes from non-renewable sources such as coal, petroleum, and natural gas.

NON-RENEWABLE means that we use these sources much faster than they re-form within the earth. We could use up our proven reserves of all of these limited energy sources within 100 years if we continue to depend on them for all of our energy needs. (A proven reserve is the amount of a natural resource that can be mined, processed, and sold at a profit.)

UNIT IV: TAKING EFFECTIVE NOTES
and
SUN, WIND, AND WATER: HOPE FOR THE FUTURE?

INTRODUCTION

In Unit III you learned that mapping helps you keep track of the important information as you read. Your map also gives you a record of the reading that you can study later.

This unit will show you two other ways to take notes, OUTLINING and making DATA TABLES.

After you have used all three forms of note taking for some time, you may find that one seems to work best for you. You may also find that each way of taking notes is more useful at some times than others.

To discover the best way for *you* to take notes in science, you need to experiment with several ways. This unit will help you do that.

NOTE TAKING TIPS

You have already learned several important skills that will help you take notes.

1. KEY WORDS — You don't need to write your notes in complete sentences. Write only the key words and phrases that tell you the main idea and important details.

2. MAIN IDEAS AND SUPPORTING DETAILS — Take notes only on the main ideas and important details. Don't try to write down everything in the reading.

Remember: Your notes are for you! Take notes in *your own words,* so that they make sense to you. You may want to use some key words from the reading, but be sure you understand what your notes say.

EXERCISE I

Directions Read the paragraph below using the four steps you learned in Unit III: SURVEY, READ, MAP, CHECK.

Keep in mind the note taking tips on page 23. Use the space below for your map.

RENEWABLE ENERGY

A report recently published by the U. S. Department of Energy (DOE) suggests that we can greatly reduce our dependence on imported oil by developing renewable energy sources. Renewable sources currently supply only 9% of the U. S. energy demand but have the potential to provide more than 250 times the amount of energy we use each year. The report also states that conversion to renewable energy sources will reduce air pollution, acid rain, and carbon dioxide emissions, which contribute to global warming.

MAP — RENEWABLE ENERGY

OUTLINING

Sometimes mapping is not the most useful way to organize your notes. OUTLINING is a way of taking notes that shows the order of events or details as they appear in your reading. The form for outlining is shown below.

OUTLINE FORM

I. Main idea
   A. Supporting detail
   B. Supporting detail
   C. Supporting detail

II. Main idea

STEPS FOR OUTLINING

Follow the steps below for taking notes in outline form.

1. Identify the main idea and supporting details of a reading or paragraph.

2. Use a Roman numeral to list the main idea.

3. Use capital letters to list the details that explain or support that main idea. Indent each capital letter to the right of the Roman numeral to set it off from the main idea.

4. Repeat as needed.

Example   Below is an outline of the paragraph you just read and mapped about "Renewable Energy."

    I. DOE report says much energy available from renewable sources

       A. Can reduce need for foreign oil

       B. Reduce air pollution, acid rain, carbon dioxide emissions

EXERCISE II

Directions   Read the rest of the passage on renewable energy on the next page. Write your notes about the reading in OUTLINE FORM in the space provided after the reading. Parts of the outline have been filled in for you.

RENEWABLE ENERGY *(continued)*

What are the renewable energy resources that hold such promise? The most important of these sources are solar, hydropower, wind, and biomass. Each of these uses the power of the sun in one way or another. Unlike oil, coal, or natural gas, they are quickly replaced no matter how much of them we use. The DOE report states that renewable sources could supply up to 30% of the U. S. energy consumption right now with existing technology and many times that with new technology. *Passive solar energy*, which depends on appropriate building design and use, could provide as much as 40% of the space heating for a home or commercial building. Active solar energy, which uses rooftop panels and pumps, could provide from 30% to 70% of needed water or space heating. Solar energy can also be used to make electricity through the use of photovoltaic cells and concentrating collectors. Electricity from solar energy is rapidly becoming competitive with fossil fuel and nuclear generation in terms of price.

The power of the *wind* can also be harnessed to produce electricity or to do mechanical work like pumping water. Where conditions are favorable, wind generation of electricity is now competitive in price with conventional methods. In California, for example, more than 15,000 wind turbines have been installed to produce electricity during the past eight years. The long-term potential for wind power is not yet known.

Hydroelectric power is the energy contained in falling water. It already provides 15% of the U. S. electricity supply and is low in cost. The DOE report states that this amount could easily be doubled. The renewable energy source with the most potential is *biomass*. Biomass is the energy contained in growing things. Wood and other plant material can be burned to produce heat. They can also be turned into methane, a burnable gas, or into alcohol, a liquid fuel. Energy from biomass may supply almost 20% of the U. S. energy supply by the year 2000, according to the DOE report, although the cost of this energy is not yet known.

OUTLINE

I. Renewable energy

    A. _____

    B. _____

II. Solar energy

III.

IV.

V.

DATA TABLES

Some readings present you with many facts about several related subjects. You may *want* to take notes on these readings that show connections between the facts, as mapping does, *and that* organize all the facts in an orderly way, as outlining does. One way to do this in one set of notes is to make a DATA TABLE from the reading.

A data table is a chart that shows the data or facts in the reading. An example of a data table of the paragraph about solar energy in the reading, "Renewable Energy," is shown below.

Example:

THREE KINDS OF SOLAR ENERGY

Energy sources	Uses	Potential	Cost
Passive solar	Space heating	40%	Very low
Active solar heating	Space, water	30%-70%	More than passive
Solar electricity	Electricity	not given	Becoming competitive

HOW TO MAKE A DATA TABLE

A DATA TABLE is most useful for taking notes on readings that give you several different pieces of information about each related topic. Follow the steps below to make a data table. Look at the example on page 27 as you read through the steps.

1. On the left hand side of your paper, identify and list the *topics* about which you have several different pieces of information.

    In the *Example* on page 27, these topics are passive solar, active solar, and solar electricity.

2. Along the top of your paper, write the *kinds of information* you have about each topic.

    In the *Example* on page 27, the information you have about each kind of solar energy includes uses, potential, and cost.

3. Draw lines between topics to make rows and between kinds of information to make columns.

4. *Fill in the information* about each topic in the appropriate boxes.

    For instance, in the *Example* on page 27, passive solar is used for space heating; active solar is used for space and water heating; and solar electricity is used for electricity.

5. Give your DATA TABLE a *title* that explains what information it contains.

    The title of the data table in the *Example* is "Three Kinds of Solar Energy."

EXERCISE III

Directions: Re-read the last three paragraphs of "Renewable Energy" on page 26. In the space provided below, make a data table of the information in those three paragraphs.

Follow the steps listed above. Use the *Example* on page 27 as a model.

_____
(title)

Energy sources	Uses	Potential	Cost

EXERCISE IV

Directions: Survey and read "Renewable Energy and Appropriate Technology" below.

In the spaces provided on the next page:

1) Take notes on the first two paragraphs in either MAP or OUTLINE form.

2) Take notes on the last three paragraphs by making a DATA TABLE of the information.

3) CHECK yourself by writing a one or two sentence summary telling what you learned from this reading.

RENEWABLE ENERGY AND APPROPRIATE TECHNOLOGY

When technologies use non-renewable sources of energy, they are limited in several ways. To begin with, oil, coal, and natural gas are usually removed from the ground in far away places, often in foreign countries. They must be shipped great distances in order to reach us. This makes them more expensive than they would be if they were available locally. Non-renewable energy sources also face shortages and sudden cutoffs that can bring the technologies dependent on them to a stop.

As non-renewable resources grow more scarce, they will become more and more expensive. One day in the not-so-distant future, the proven reserves may run out. From then on, the technologies that used them will be useless.

Appropriate technologies avoid these limitations by drawing their power from renewable energy sources whenever possible. For example, consider the differences between a house heated by a non-renewable fuel like natural gas and a similar house heated primarily by the sun. The house using natural gas for heat depends on a constant supply to stay warm. If there is a shortage of natural gas caused by a very cold winter or by a shipping problem, the gas heated house may become too cold for comfort if its supply runs out before the problem is solved. The solar heated house, on the other hand, cannot be cut off from its main fuel supply for more than a few days at a time.

The owner of the gas heated house will have to spend more and more money for natural gas every year. The cost goes up as the proven reserves of natural gas get smaller and the cost of shipping increases. In contrast, the house equipped with solar technology has small, stable energy costs. The owner of the solar heated house will only have to spend money for heat during periods of cloudy weather.

The day will come when the natural gas reserves are nearly gone. On that day the owner of the gas heated house will have to replace his or her gas fired furnace with a more appropriate technology. Chances are it will run on renewable energy.

1) MAP or OUTLINE of paragraphs 1 and 2:

2) DATA TABLE of paragraphs 3, 4, and 5.

_____
(title)

Kind of heat in house	Shortages and cutoffs	Costs	Future

3) CHECK: _____

_____

_____

_____

UNIT IV SUMMARY

TAKING NOTES

There is no one right way to take notes. Different note taking methods are appropriate in different situations. You may be more comfortable taking notes in a certain way.

The important part of taking notes is to record the main ideas and supporting details in a way that makes them easy for you to understand and remember.

TIPS: 1. Only write down key words and phrases, not complete sentences.

2. Take notes on main ideas and supporting details. Don't try to record everything.

3. Take notes in your own words, so that they make sense to you.

OUTLINING is a way of taking notes that shows the order in which events happened. It can also show which supporting detail comes before another. This is an OUTLINE FORM:

I. Main idea
   A. Supporting detail
   B. Supporting detail
   C. Supporting detail

II. Main idea

Making a DATA TABLE is helpful when a reading gives you several pieces of information about more than one topic. The data table shows you how each topic is the same or different from the others. A data table might look like this:

RENEWABLE ENERGY

Energy source	Uses	Advantages	Disadvantages
Thermal solar power	heat hot water	small, fixed costs usually available	
Hydropower	electricity	small, fixed costs renewable	have to be near falling water
Wind power	electricity mechanical work	small, fixed costs renewable	need wind

RENEWABLE ENERGY

The United States Department of Energy believes that the use of renewable energy is one solution to our energy problems. By the year 2010, at least 30% of our energy needs could be met by using renewable energy sources, of which we have a nearly unlimited supply.

The renewable energy sources with the greatest promise for the future are:
1) solar energy—use of the sun's rays for space and water heating and to generate electricity;
2) wind power—harnessing the power of the wind to generate electricity and do mechanical work;
3) hydropower—use of the energy stored in falling water to generate electricity; and
4) biomass—use of the energy stored in plant materials.

Appropriate technologies use renewable energy whenever possible to avoid shortages and cutoffs. Renewable energy is replaced almost as fast as it is used.

UNIT V: MAKING JUDGMENTS
and
HOW DOES TECHNOLOGY AFFECT THE ENVIRONMENT?

INTRODUCTION

The appropriateness of a technology depends in part on how it affects the ENVIRONMENT in which it is used.

The ENVIRONMENT includes all of the land, water, and living things (plants, animals, people) in an area. In the desert, the environment includes sand, air, cacti, snakes, people, and so on. On the coast of Iceland, the environment includes air, snow, ice, tundra, seals, fish, and so on.

A technology is most appropriate when it does not hurt or change the environment.

EXERCISE I

Directions: Below are sketches of five houses. The houses are very much the same. Five people live in each, and each is designed and insulated in the same way. Each house is heated in a different way. The words under the drawings tell what form of energy technology is used to heat each house.

On the line provided below each house, rate each house as to how its energy use affects the environment. Use a scale of 1 to 10 to rate the houses. A rating of 1 means the house's heating system does little to hurt the environment. A rating of 10 means the system does great harm to the environment. Use the numbers 1 through 10 to show how much you think the energy use in each house affects the environment.

HOUSE A	HOUSE B	HOUSE C	HOUSE D	HOUSE E
Heated by electricity	Heated by burning coal	Heated by burning natural gas	Heated with oil	Passive solar heat and wood burning stove.

RATING ON A SCALE OF 1 TO 10:

_____   _____   _____   _____   _____

MAKING JUDGMENTS: FACT AND OPINION

How did you decide on a rating for each house in Exercise I? Did you have the information you needed to make a good decision?

Making good choices or judgments often depends on having the facts. Without facts, you may end up basing your choice on opinion only.

A *fact* is something (events, pieces of information, data) that is accepted as true.

An *opinion* is a person's idea or belief. People may have different opinions or interpretations of the same event, data, or experience.

Example: *Fact:*   John has brown hair.
Opinion: John's hair is beautiful.

Fact: The sun will set at 7:02 p.m.
Opinion: My view of the sunset is better than yours.

EXERCISE II

Directions: Below are five sentences about strip mining for coal. Each sentence is either a fact or an opinion. In the space provided next to each sentence, write *fact* if you think it is a fact, or *opinion* if you think it is an opinion.

_____ 1. Strip mining is the least expensive way to remove coal from the earth.

_____ 2. The least expensive way is always the best for everyone.

_____ 3. In strip mining, soil and rock are stripped away so that the coal can be collected.

_____ 4. It often takes thousands of years before dry areas that have been strip mined return to their natural condition.

_____ 5. Coal is the most valuable resource in the U.S. today.

MAKING JUDGMENTS: USING CRITERIA

Once you have found the facts that will help you make a judgment, you need a way of comparing them. It is useful to develop CRITERIA or standards against which you can judge your information.

Example: Below are 4 *criteria* useful in judging how different kinds of energy technology affect the environment.

1. The technology should have little immediate or long term effect on living things.
2. The technology should not make the environment smell or look unpleasant.
3. The environment should be able to recover quickly from the technology.
4. The technology should not produce a lot of waste material.

EXERCISE III

Directions: On the lines provided, write two criteria for each of the following items:

A really good milkshake

1. _____

_____

2. _____

_____

A safe bicycle

1. _____

_____

2. _____

_____

EXERCISE IV

Directions: Your teacher will give you some facts about each house that you rated in Exercise I. Each set of facts includes information about the effects of the energy technology used on the environment.

Read the information about each house. As a group, rate each house again on its effect on the environment. This time, use the facts you have been given and the criteria listed above in making your judgments. Put your ratings on the lines under the houses below.

Use the same rating system you used in Exercise I to rate the houses. On a scale of 1 to 10, 1 means a house that does little to damage the environment, and 10 means a house that harms the environment a great deal.

HOUSE A	HOUSE B	HOUSE C	HOUSE D	HOUSE E
Heated by electricity	Heated by burning coal	Heated by burning natural gas	Heated with oil	Passive solar heat and wood burning stove.

RATING ON A SCALE OF 1 TO 10:

_____   _____   _____   _____   _____

UNIT V SUMMARY

MAKING JUDGMENTS

To make good decisions or judgments, you need to have *facts* so that your decision is not based on *opinion* alone.

A *fact* is something that is accepted as true. Data that you gather in science are facts.

An *opinion* is a person's idea or belief. Once you have facts or data, you can make interpretations or form opinions.

You also need to have *criteria* that serve as standards against which you can judge the facts you gather. Facts give you the information you need. Criteria help you use the facts to make judgments or decisions.

APPROPRIATE TECHNOLOGY AND THE ENVIRONMENT

The *environment is* the land, water, and living things in a particular area. *A* technology is most appropriate when it does not hurt or change the environment.

Four criteria for judging whether or not a technology is appropriate in its effects on the environment are:

1. The technology has little short or long term effect on living things.

2. The technology does not make the environment smell or look unpleasant.

3. The environment can recover from the technology quickly.

4. The technology does not produce a lot of waste material.

UNIT VI: WORKING WITH GRAPHS
and
HOW CAN WE USE ENERGY EFFICIENTLY?

INTRODUCTION

Look at the sketch below.

In the space provided on page 38, explain what you think this device does. Then list two things that are wrong with this device.

This device _____

_____

Two things wrong with this device are:

1) _____

_____

2) _____

_____

ENTROPY AND EFFICIENCY

In the E-Z Window Opener in the Introduction, human energy from someone's arm is turned into mechanical energy to open the window. But some of the energy used to pull down the short lever had to be used to lift the side of the bucket. Some energy was used to overcome friction, or the resistance that occurs when two objects rub together. This energy did nothing to open the window. It was turned into heat, and did no work. This loss of energy as it changes from one form to another is an example of ENTROPY.

It is impossible to convert energy from one form to another or transfer it from one place to another without losing some. But some technologies waste more energy than others. If much entropy occurs, the process used to convert energy is not EFFICIENT.

This unit will show you how information about energy efficiency can help you decide whether or not a technology is appropriate.

EXERCISE I

Directions The picture on the next page represents a common way to burn oil to produce electricity. The electricity is then used to heat water. Entropy occurs here, just as it did in the E-Z Window Opener.

The paragraphs below the picture describe what happens in the picture. Read the paragraphs. Each time you come to a number in parentheses ( ) in the paragraphs, write that number in the appropriate place in the picture. Each number shows where entropy is taking place.

When you are done, answer the question below the paragraphs on page 39.

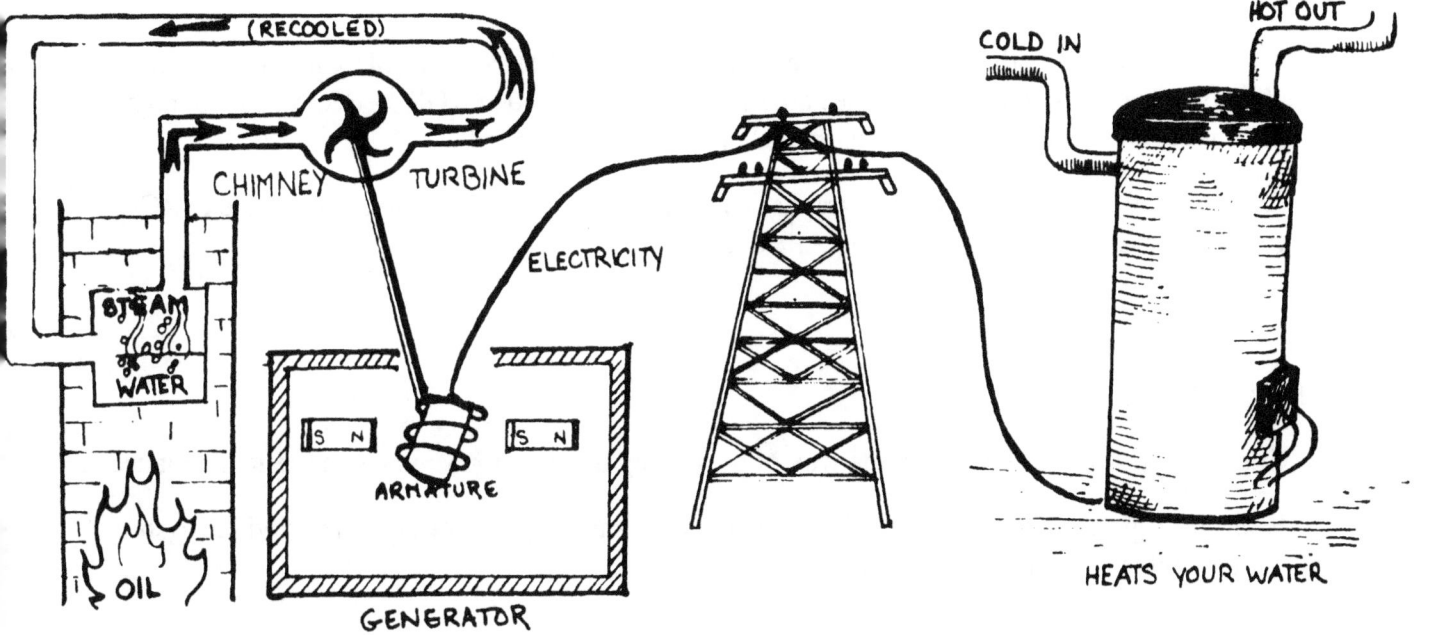

OIL TO ELECTRICITY TO HOT WATER

Three gallons of oil must be burned at the power plant to deliver the energy of one gallon of oil to your house. Two-thirds of the energy in the oil is lost when it is converted to electricity and transported to your house.

When oil is burned, only a part of the heat goes into the water at the power plant. Much of the heat goes up the chimney (1), and some goes to heat the container holding the water (2). As the water changes to steam, some of its heat is used to heat the pipes it passes through (3). When the steam turns the turbine, it must overcome friction (4). Energy is also used to overcome friction as it turns the armature (5). As the electricity created in the generator travels through wires from the power plant to your house, some of the electricity escapes from the wires into the air (6). Some heats the wires (7). At your house, most electricity you receive is used to heat the water.

Explain one way you might be able to avoid energy loss in the process shown above.

___

___

___

___

___

GRAPHS

As you may have already discovered, science often uses numbers as a way of explaining important ideas. In order to compare the numbers, they are sometimes organized into GRAPHS. As you found out in Unit V, you can become a better decision maker by comparing facts.

There are several different kinds of graphs. This unit will show you how to read and use CIRCLE GRAPHS, BAR GRAPHS, and LINE GRAPHS about energy efficiency.

CIRCLE GRAPHS

Circle graphs, or pie charts, are one way of presenting information so you can see it at a glance.

Each circle graph equals all, or 100%, of whatever it is showing. The circle can be divided to show parts, or percentages, of the whole amount.

Example: This circle graph shows what portion of the oil burned in the power plant is actually used to heat water in your home.

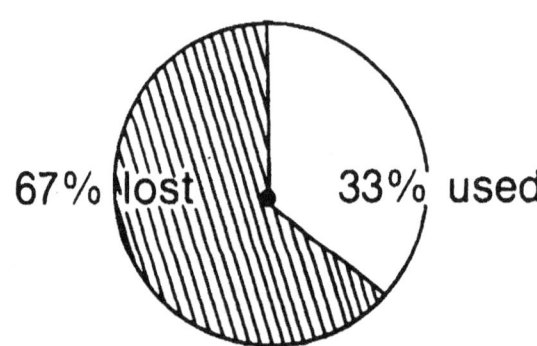

- The whole circle, 100%, is the amount of energy the power plant starts with.

- The shaded area represents the portion or percentage of the energy lost in the process.

- The unshaded area shows the portion or percentage of the oil actually used to heat your water at home.

EXERCISE II

Directions: Below are circle graphs that show how much energy is actually used and how much is lost in five different technologies.

1) Shade the "energy loss" section of each graph.

2) Write in the percentage of energy loss on each graph.

3) Answer the questions on the next page that ask you to compare the technologies shown in the graphs.

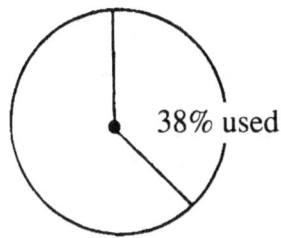

Average fossil fuel converted to electricity

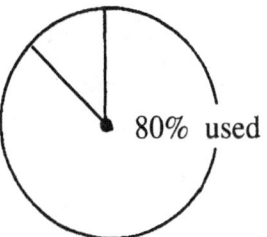

Oil (converted to heat) burned in an efficient furnace

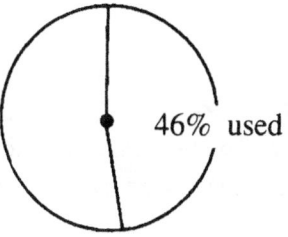

Steam engine (water converted to mechanical energy)

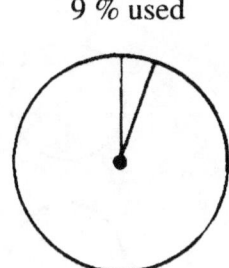

Gasoline burned in an automobile (gas converted to mechanical energy)

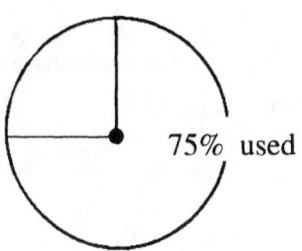

Natural gas converted to heat in an efficient furnace

QUESTIONS

1. How much energy is actually used when oil is converted to heat? _____

2. How much energy is lost when natural gas is converted to heat? _____

3. Which energy technology shown on page 41 is the most efficient (wastes the least energy)?
   _____

4. Which two technologies are the least efficient? _____
   _____

5. Explain one way you could cut down on your use of one of the least efficient energy technologies shown on page 41. _____
   _____
   _____
   _____

EXERCISE III

Directions: Below is some information about the amount of energy used and lost by different sectors of society in the U.S.

Using the circle next to each set of information, make a circle graph that shows energy used and lost in each area of society. To measure the size of each section, start at the top of the circle and work clockwise. Draw the lines needed to mark the two sections, "used" and "lost." Then shade in the section of each graph that shows how much energy is lost.

1. Residential (home) energy use: 76% used / 24% lost
2. Commercial energy use (stores, restaurants, schools):   76% used / 24% lost
3. Industrial energy use: 75% used / 25% lost
4. Transportation energy use: 27% used / 73% lost
5. Generation of electricity: 33% used / 67% lost

BAR GRAPHS

Each circle graph shows you one set of information at a time. With a BAR GRAPH you can compare several different pieces of information according to the same standard.

In a BAR GRAPH the standard is presented along the left hand side of the paper. The pieces of information are shown along the bottom. Each bar shows where along the standard the information falls.

Example: The bar graph below shows some of the same information presented on the circle graphs in Exercise III, page 41. It shows the percentage of energy lost in each sector of society. The bar graph lets you compare the efficiency of energy use of the different sectors.

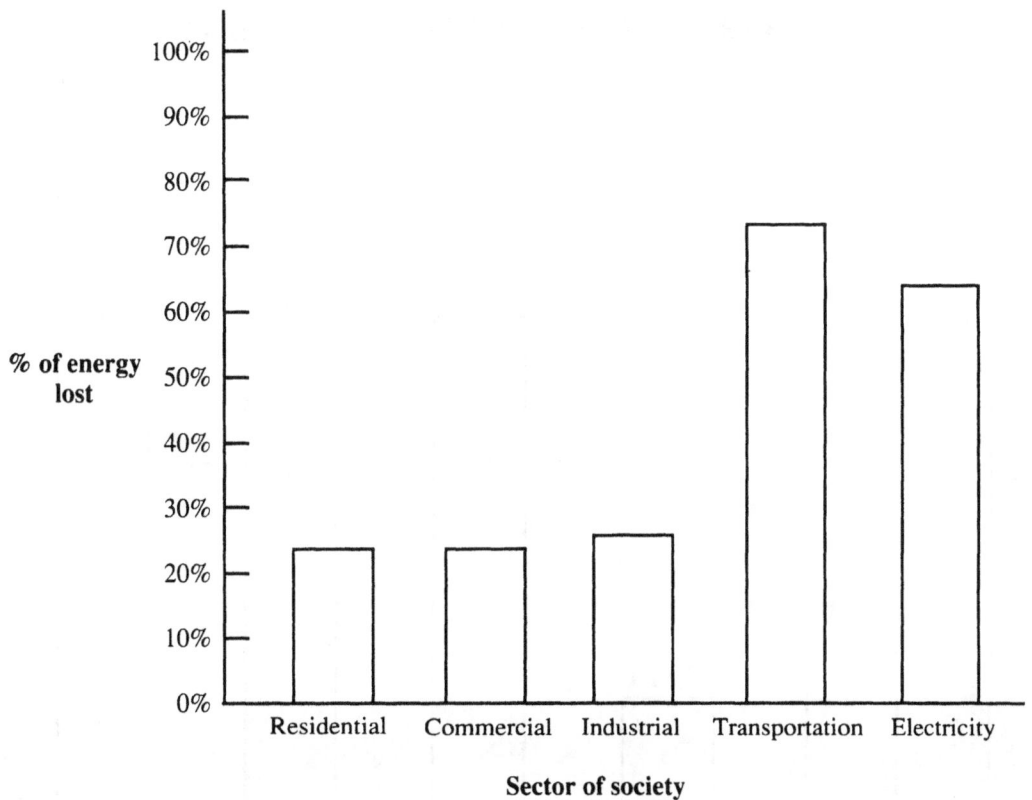

- The left side of the graph is divided into percentages of energy lost. This is the standard.

- The bottom of the graph shows each sector of society that uses energy.

- Each bar shows the percentage of energy lost in each sector of society.

EXERCISE IV

Directions: The bar graph below shows the actual amounts of energy each sector of society uses. The left side of the graph is divided into trillions of BTUs, or British Thermal Units. A BTU is the amount of energy needed to raise the temperature of one pound of water one degree Fahrenheit. Each bar shows how many BTUs each sector of society uses.

Below the graph are numbers that tell you how many BTUs of energy are lost by each sector of society.

Using this information, shade in the part of each bar that will show how much of the total energy used by each sector of society is lost. The residential sector bar has been done as an example. Then answer the questions about the graph on page 45.

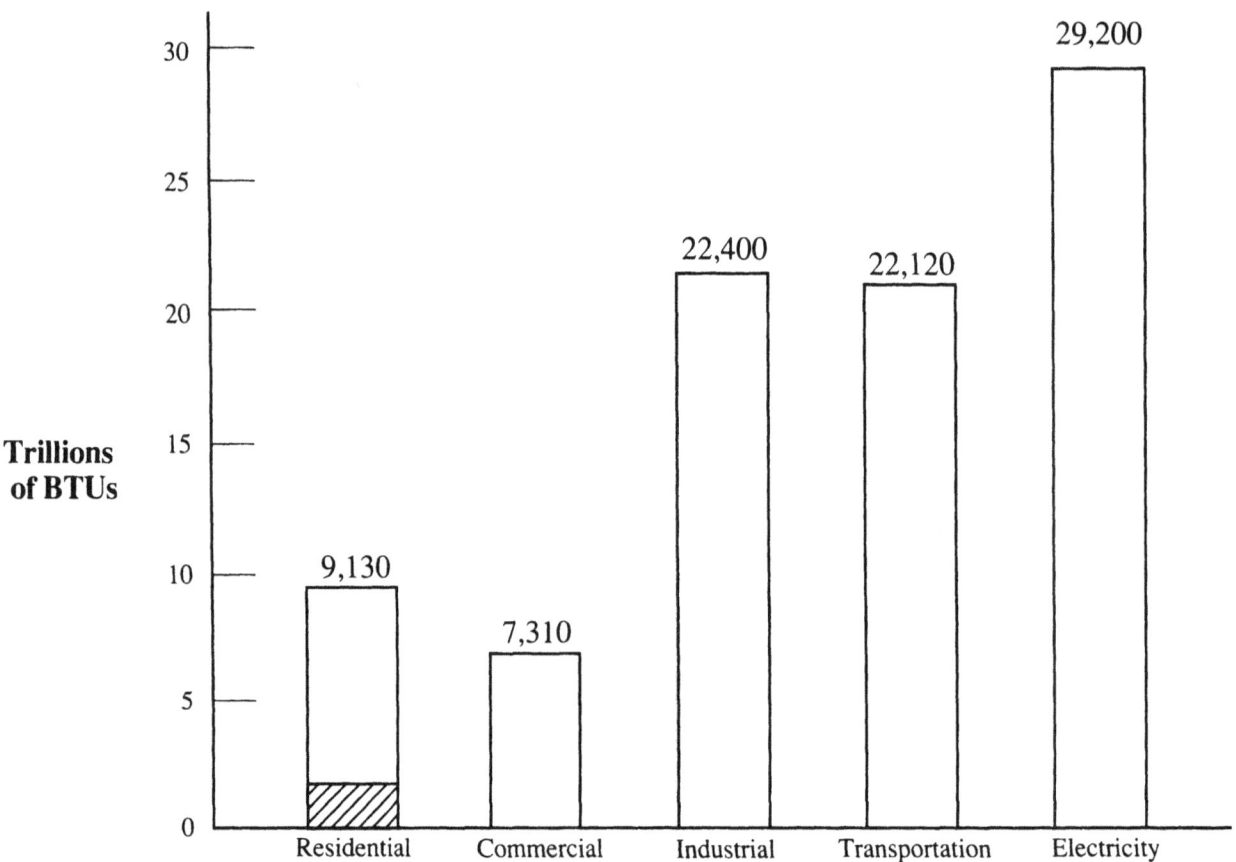

ENERGY USED BY SECTORS OF SOCIETY

	Energy lost	**In trillions of BTUs**
Residential sector	24%	2,191
Commercial sector	24%	1,754
Industrial sector	25%	5,500
Transportation sector	73%	16,148
Electricity generation	67%	19,564

QUESTIONS

1. Which sector of society uses the most energy? _____

2. Which sector of society uses the least energy? _____

3. Which two sectors of society are least efficient in their energy use? _____
   _____

4. Which sector of society uses energy most efficiently? _____
   _____

LINE GRAPHS

A third type of graph is a LINE GRAPH. A line graph is built on two sets of information, one presented along the left side or *vertical axis* of the graph, and one shown along the bottom or *horizontal axis* of the graph. Each point on the graph shows you two pieces of information.

By connecting related points on a line graph, you can see how the information changes over time or is related to other information.

Example: The line graph below shows the amount of energy used in the residential and commercial sectors of society in the U.S. between 1950 and 1989. The graph is explained on the next page. Look at the graph as you read through this explanation.

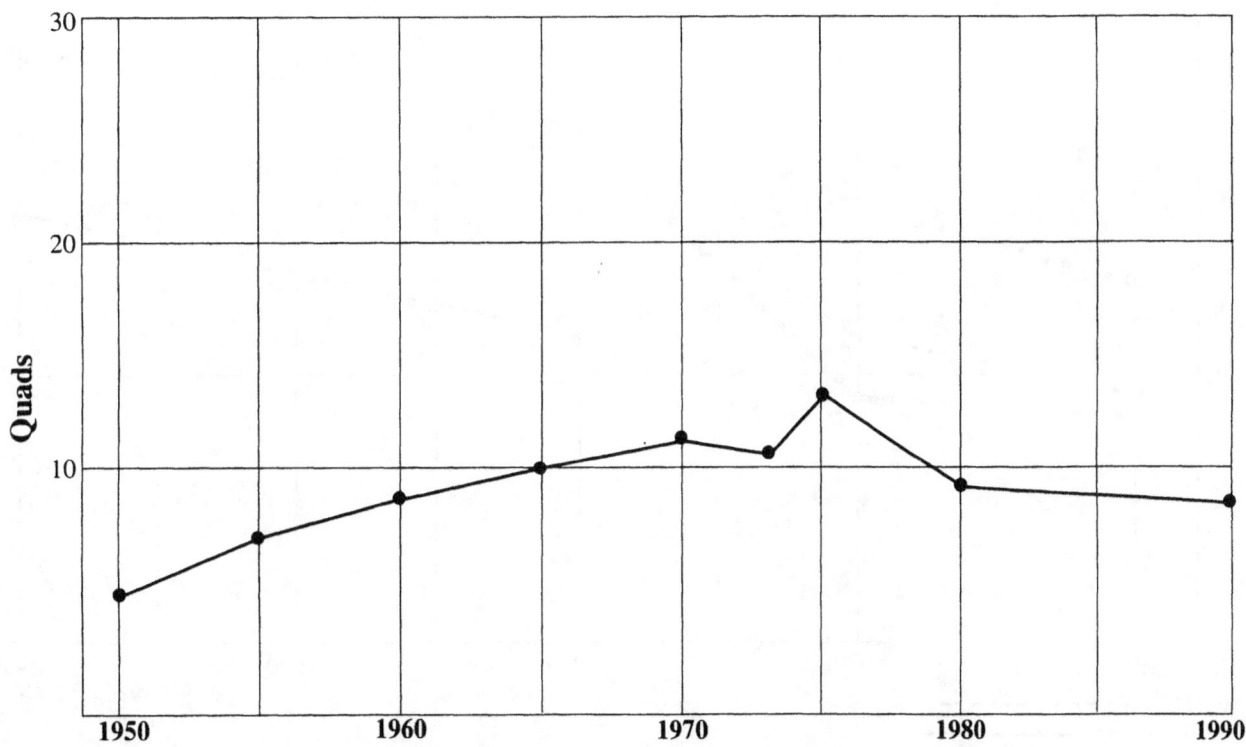

ENERGY USE IN RESIDENTIAL SECTOR

Explanation

- The left side (vertical axis) of the graph shows energy use in quads. A quad equals one quadrillion BTUs.

- The bottom line (horizontal axis) of the graph shows the years between 1950 and 1990.

- The line on the graph shows the change in the number of quads of energy used in the residential sector between 1950 and 1990.

To find out how much energy the residential sector of society used in any one year, find that year on the horizontal axis of the graph. Use a straight edge to find the place on the line directly above the year on the horizontal axis. Mark that point. Then use a straight edge to find the point on the vertical axis directly to the left of the point you have marked on the line. That number on the vertical axis is the number of quads of energy used in the residential sector in the year you are looking at.

For example, in 1960, the residential sector used about 8 quads of energy.

EXERCISE V

Directions: The graph below is similar to the graph in the *Example* on page 45, except that it shows energy use in four different sectors of society: residential and commercial, industrial, transportation, and electricity.

Look over the graph to see what it tells you. Then use the graph to help you answer the questions on page 47.

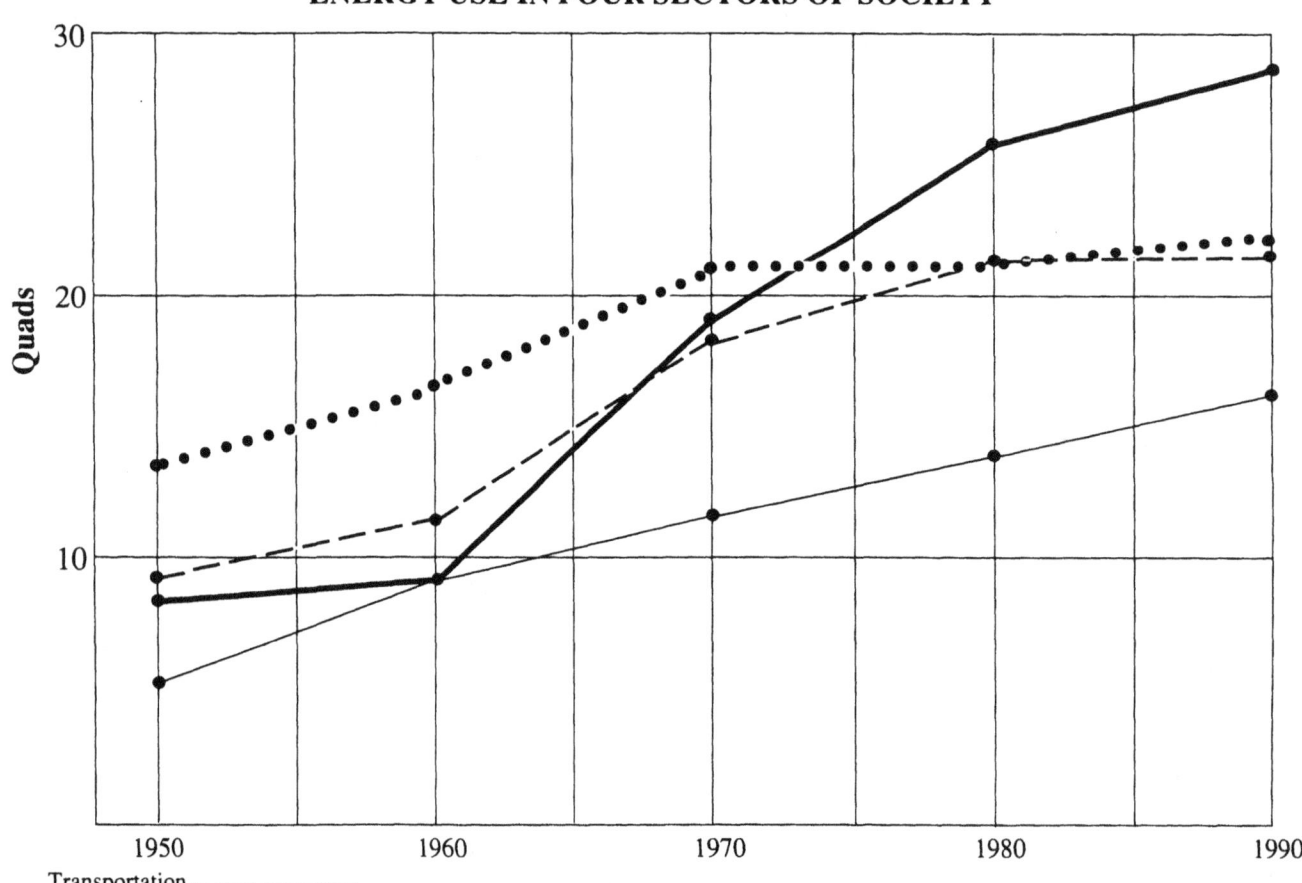

ENERGY USE IN FOUR SECTORS OF SOCIETY

Transportation — — — — —
Electric utilities ─────
Industrial and miscellaneous • • • • • • •
Residential and commercial ─────

QUESTIONS

1. Which sector used the most energy in 1978? _____

2. Which sector used the least energy in 1978? _____

3. About how many quads of energy did the transportation sector of society use in 1970? _____
   _____

4. Which sector of society had the biggest increase in energy use between 1960 and 1989? (Subtract the number of quads of energy used in 1960 from the number used in 1989. The sector in which the number is biggest increased its energy use the most.)
   _____

5. Explain one thing the U.S. might do to decrease its energy use in the sector of society that uses the most energy.

   _____

   _____

   _____

UNIT VI SUMMARY

GRAPHS

Graphs are pictures that let you see a lot of information at once. Graphs also help you compare pieces of information so you can make decisions or judgments about them.

CIRCLE GRAPHS are circles divided into parts.

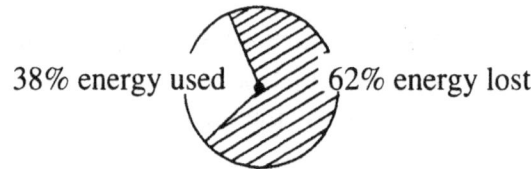

BAR GRAPHS put information into a form that lets you compare.

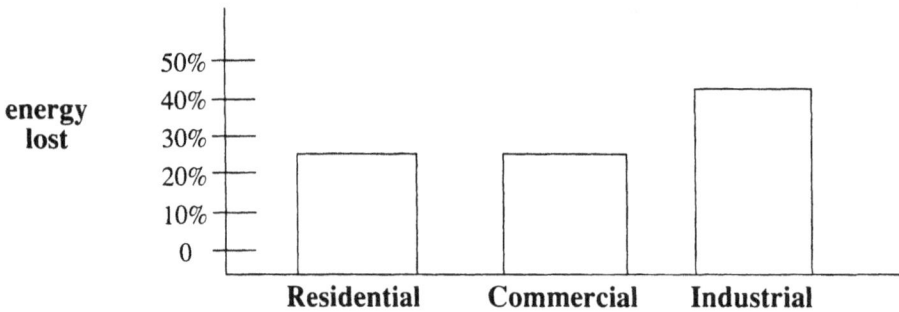

LINE GRAPHS present the changes in information over time.

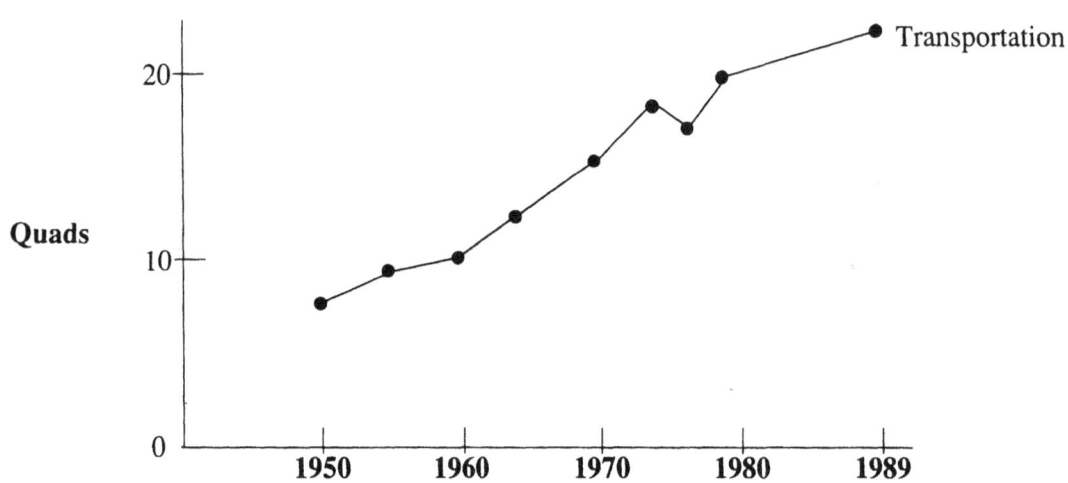

ENERGY EFFICIENCY

Efficiency is an important consideration in judging the appropriateness of a technology and choosing which technology is appropriate.

When converting energy from one form to another, energy is often lost through ENTROPY. Energy use is most efficient where the least entropy occurs.

All sectors of society have some entropy. The most entropy occurs in the transportation and electrical generation sectors. It is in these sectors especially that we must develop more efficient energy use.

UNIT VII: SOLVING PROBLEMS
and
HOW MUCH DO TECHNOLOGIES COST?

INTRODUCTION

Your teacher will ask three of you to read the conversation below aloud. As you listen and follow along, think about what Lisa's problem is and how she might go about solving it. After the conversation has been read, write your ideas in the space provided.

LISA'S PROBLEM

Mother: Lisa, the local newspaper called today to say that your application for a weekend paper route has been approved.

Lisa: Oh great! I thought they'd never get around to calling me. How soon do I have to let them know I want it?

Mother: By next Monday.

Lisa: That's no problem.

Mother: Well, I don't know. How do you plan to deliver all those papers every weekend? You know I won't be able to drive you around the neighborhood in the car, and it's too much walking with all that weight.

Lisa: I've got that all figured out, Mom. I can take some money out of my savings account and buy a new bicycle with it.

Father: Now hold on! You're supposed to be saving that money for college.

Lisa: Oh, Dad! I can replace it out of the money I earn from the paper route, plus put in a whole lot more.

Mother: Just how much do you plan on spending for this bicycle?

Lisa: Well, there's this great ten speed on sale down at the Bike Hut for only $200.

Mother: Oh, Lisa! That's way too much money to spend on just a bicycle.

Lisa: Come on, Mother! It's a great bike.

Father: Wait a minute, Lisa. How much did you say you would earn if you take the route?

Lisa: It's $10 a week, and it goes up every year. Roberto's already making $12 a week, and it's only his third year.

Father: Well, let's see. That makes $520 the first year, about $45 each month. If you add on the cost of the bicycle license and normal maintenance, it will take you almost half of the year to earn back all the money you want to take out of your savings account. And that doesn't count the interest you would earn if you left the money in the bank.

Mother: Why don't you find a used bicycle for less money? That way you'd make a profit much sooner.

Lisa: You're probably right, Mom. But I'd rather not ride around town on some old heap. That's too depressing even to think about.

Father: Lisa, I think you need to investigate this idea more carefully before we can make a decision. Why don't we talk about it again in a few days after you've gathered the necessary information?

Lisa: Do I have to?

Mother: I think it would be best, Lisa.

Lisa: All right. I'll see what I can do. But it won't be easy.

What is Lisa's problem? _____

_____

_____

_____

How should she go about solving it? _____

_____

_____

_____

PROBLEM SOLVING

Imagine trying to get somewhere you have never been before without a map or a set of directions. You would wander around not knowing which way to turn or how far to go. If you were lucky, you might end up where you wanted to be, but you would have wasted time and energy along the way. A map or directions would help you get there much more easily.

Problem solving is the same way. You start with a question, and you end with an answer. If you have a map or a plan for solving the problem, you will be more successful at finding the answer.

In this unit you will learn one possible plan you can use to help you solve problems in science. The plan is made up of these five steps, each of which will be explained later in the unit:

>POSING THE QUESTION
>SELECTING DATA
>GATHERING DATA
>ORGANIZING DATA
>DRAWING CONCLUSIONS

STEP TWO: SELECTING DATA

Now that you know what the problem is and have stated it in the form of a question, you are ready for the next step.

If you had to travel all the way across town to a friend's house where you had never been before, you would need information in order to get there. You would need to know names of streets, turns to make, and distances to travel.

Problem solving is similar. There are certain pieces of information, or DATA, that you need to answer the question posed in Step One. In Step Two, SELECTING DATA, you identify the pieces of information you need and decide where to look for them.

EXERCISE II

Directions: Working with your group, list the pieces of information Lisa needs to answer the question your class has posed for her. Next to each piece of information on the list, write where you think Lisa can get that information. Use the space below to make your lists. Keep in mind the life cycle costs (use, maintenance, replacement) described above.

INFORMATION NEEDED   **WHERE TO GET IT**

_____   _____

_____   _____

_____   _____

_____   _____

_____   _____

_____   _____

_____   _____

_____   _____

_____   _____

_____   _____

STEP ONE: POSING THE QUESTION

In the first step in problem solving, you have to take aim on the problem, just like a sharpshooter takes aim on the target before firing. You must know *exactly* what question you are trying to answer *right from the start,* or you may waste valuable time.

The first step in solving a problem, then, is to ask yourself, "What exactly do I want to find out?"

EXERCISE I

Directions: Re-read the conversation on pages 49-50 between Lisa and her parents. Then work with your group to decide exactly what Lisa's problem is. Write the problem in the form of a question on the lines below.

_____

_____

_____

_____

_____

LIFE CYCLE COST

In Unit V, you learned that it was useful to have criteria in making judgments. Criteria are also useful in helping to solve problems. In solving Lisa's problem, a key criterion is the life cycle cost of the bicycle she will buy.

When you go to buy a product or a piece of machinery, you usually look at how much it costs before you buy it. That is the product's *first cost.* But you also need to think about other hidden costs before you make your decision.

The *life cycle cost* of the product or machine is how much it will cost during the time that you own and use it. This includes whatever it costs to *buy* it, to *use* it, to *maintain* it or keep it running, and eventually to *replace* it when it wears out.

The life cycle cost of a product or machine will be lowest if the product is:

> *durable*—it will last a long time, and

> *reliable*—it doesn't need much maintenance or repair.

A technology is more appropriate if its life cycle cost is low, that is, if it is durable and reliable. Lisa needs to find out which bicycle will have the lower life cycle cost so that she can answer her question.

STEP THREE: GATHERING DATA

Once you know what it is you are trying to find out (POSING THE QUESTION) and what pieces of information you need in order to come up with an answer (SELECTING DATA), you are ready for Step Three: GATHERING DATA.

GATHERING DATA means collecting the information you need and writing it down clearly and neatly so you can read and use it later. You don't need to figure out the answer to your problem yet. Just collect and record the pieces of information you need.

EXERCISE III

Directions: Read the conversations below with your group. Then go back through each conversation and write down the information given that you will need to answer Lisa's question. Use the space provided after the conversations to write down your information. Be sure all information is clearly labeled.

Use the list you wrote on page 52 to help you keep track of information you need.

LISA GATHERS INFORMATION

Scene: The Bike Hut

Lisa:	Excuse me, can you help me please?
Salesperson:	I'll try. What are you looking for?
Lisa:	Well, actually I need some information. Is that blue ten speed in the window still on sale?
Sales:	Yes. It will sell for $200 through next Friday. Then it goes back up to $275. Are you thinking of buying it?
Lisa:	I'm not sure yet. Can you give me some idea of how much I'd have to spend in order to keep it in good shape and the cost of a license and things like that?
Sales:	You mean the life cycle cost?
Lisa:	What's that?
Sales:	The cost of buying, using, maintaining, and eventually replacing your bicycle.
Lisa:	Yes, I guess I need to know the life cycle cost.
Sales:	Okay. To begin with, a bicycle license costs $15 no matter what bike you buy.
Lisa:	Will I have to buy a new one each year?
Sales:	No, just once. As far as maintenance goes, it's not bad at all. It will vary from year to year, but if you take good care of it, you shouldn't have to spend more than $25 a year to keep it in working order.
Lisa:	That's great! How long do you think it would last before I'd have to replace it?
Sales:	Oh, ten years at least. Now, were you thinking about getting some insurance?
Lisa:	No, why?

Sales: A lot of ten speeds have been stolen around town lately. You can insure the bike you're interested in for only $10 a year. That way, if it's stolen, you'll have enough money to replace it.

Lisa: I think I've got all that down. Now, my mother wants me to find out about a used bike, too. Just in case the ten speed is too much.

Sales: We have a pretty good one in the back for only $75, but I don't think it will last more than four years.

Lisa: How much do you think I would have to spend a year to keep that one going?

Sales: Probably around $60. But you'd have to rent a replacement bike while the used one was in the shop being fixed. That would cost around $25 a year.

Lisa: A used bike sure doesn't sound like a good idea.

Sales: Well, it all depends on what you plan to use it for.

Lisa: A paper route.

Sales: Well, that would certainly wear it out fast. You'd end up having to replace it after four years. By then, a ten speed bike like the one in the window will probably cost around $350.

Lisa: Well, that tells me all I need to know. I'll let you know what I decide. Thanks for your help.

Sales: You're welcome. Good luck!

* * * * * * * * *

Scene: The local newspaper office

Editor: What can I do for you, Miss?

Lisa: I'm trying to find out how much I'll make a week if I take the weekend paper route your paper has offered me.

Sales Manager: That's easy. $10 a week your first year, $11 your second, $12 your third, and $13 your fourth. Keeps going up a dollar a year.

Lisa: That's it?

Sales Manager: Yep, except for tips from your customers, but you shouldn't count on that.

Lisa: Okay. Thanks a lot.

Sales Manager: Any time.

* * * * * * * * *

Scene: Lisa's bank

Lisa: Can you tell me how much interest I would lose in a year if I withdrew $200 from my savings account?

Teller: Yes, that would probably be about $10.

Lisa: How about if I only withdrew $75?

Teller: Then it's about $3.75 in interest.

Lisa: Thank you very much.

* * * * * * * * *

INFORMATION GATHERED FROM LISA'S CONVERSATIONS:

STEP FOUR: ORGANIZING DATA

Now that you have gathered your data, you may be tempted to jump right in and start drawing conclusions. Beware! Unless you have organized your data, you may be wasting your time.

The fourth step in problem solving is ORGANIZING DATA by putting it into a chart or graph that helps you make sense out of it. Organizing the information often shows you patterns or ideas that will lead you to the answer you are looking for.

Example: Below is a data table that organizes the information Lisa gathered about the two bicycles at the Bike Hut.

Data Table #1

COST OF BICYCLES

	Used Bicycle	New Bicycle
Useful life	3 years	10 years
Purchase price	$75	$200
Unearned interest (on money withdrawn from bank) (each year)	$3.75	$10
License	$15	$15
Insurance (each year)	0	$10
Maintenance (each year)	$60	$25
Rental bike during repair (each year)	$25	0
Replacement cost at end of 4 years	$350 (for a new bike)	0
TOTAL COST after 1 year	$178.75	$260
TOTAL COST after 2 years	$267.50	$305
TOTAL COST after 3 years	$356.25	$350
TOTAL COST after 4 years (includes replacement cost)	$795.00	$395

EXERCISE IV

Directions: Below and on page 57 are two more data tables to help you organize the data you have gathered about Lisa's problem. The data table "EARNINGS FROM WEEKEND NEWSPAPER ROUTE" has been completed for you.

Use Data Table #1 in the *Example* on page 55 and Data Table #2 below to complete Data Table on the next page: "PROFIT FROM NEWSPAPER ROUTE." You will find the information you need about *cost* in Data Table #1 and the information about *earnings* in Data Table #2.

Costs come from the total costs at the bottom of Data Table #1, "COST OF BICYCLES."

Earnings come from the Cumulative Pay column of Data Table #2, "EARNINGS FROM WEEKEND NEWSPAPER ROUTE."

Profit = Earnings minus Costs.

Data Table #2

EARNINGS FROM WEEKEND NEWSPAPER ROUTE

Year	Weekly Pay	Yearly Pay	Cumulative Pay*
1	$10	$520	$520
2	$11	$572	$1,092
3	$12	$624	$1,716
4	$13	$676	$2,392

*Cumulative pay is the total amount Lisa has earned at the end of each year. It includes all the money she has earned that year *plus* all her earnings from the year(s) before.

Data Table #3

PROFIT FROM NEWSPAPER ROUTE

Time	Item	Used Bicycle	New Bicycle
End of 1st year	Earnings		
	Cost		
	Profit		
End of 2nd year	Earnings		
	Cost		
	Profit		
End of 3rd year	Earnings		
	Cost		
	Profit		
End of 4th year	Earnings		
	Cost		
	Profit		

STEP FIVE: DRAWING CONCLUSIONS

So far, in solving Lisa's problem, you have

POSED THE QUESTION,

SELECTED DATA you needed to answer the question,

GATHERED DATA needed to answer the question, and

ORGANIZED DATA in a way that allows possible patterns in the data to catch your eye.

Perhaps you have already noticed a pattern within the data you have organized. The word *pattern* suggests repetition, like the pattern on wallpaper. The same picture or idea keeps reappearing as you look at it.

Data can repeat itself in the same way. As you look at the data you have collected and organized, try to find facts that fit together to form a pattern or a complete picture.

To DRAW A CONCLUSION or solve your problem, ask yourself the same question you posed back in Step One. Then look for the patterns in your organized data. If an answer to your question exists, that's where you are most likely to find it.

EXERCISE V

Directions: Turn back to page 57, and examine Lisa's third data table. Look for patterns in the data that will help you answer the question you posed in Step One.

Write your answer to that question and your reasons for choosing that answer on the lines below. Keep in mind the ideas of *first cost, life cycle cost, durability,* and *reliability* in making your decision.

Answer to question posed in Step One (on page 51): _____

_____

_____

_____

Reasons for choosing that answer: _____

_____

_____

_____

_____

LISA CHOOSES A BICYCLE

Father: Well, Lisa, what did you find out?

Lisa: To begin with, Mom was right about that used bike. It would pay for itself faster than the new one.

Mother: I had a feeling it would.

Father: I guess that settles it.

Lisa: I don't think so, Dad.

Father: Why not?

Lisa: Because I also found out that the new bike will allow me to make more money in the long run. Look at this data table and I'll show you what I mean.

Mother: Yes, I do see what you mean. I guess it just goes to show that durability can be just as important as how much something costs.

Lisa: What do you think, Dad?

Father: I think you better hurry down to the Bike Hut and buy that new ten speed before the sale ends!

UNIT VII SUMMARY

PROBLEM SOLVING

Solving problems is easier when you have a plan or set of directions that helps you get from the problem to an answer. One possible plan is to follow these five steps:

1) POSE THE QUESTION: Figure out exactly what the problem is and put it into question form.

2) SELECT THE DATA: Decide what pieces of information or data you need to solve the problem and where you can find them.

3) GATHER DATA: Find and write down the information you need to solve the problem or answer the question.

4) ORGANIZE DATA: Use data tables, graphs, or charts to help you put the information together so you can see patterns in the data.

5) DRAW CONCLUSIONS: Look for patterns in your organized data, and answer the question you posed in Step One.

APPROPRIATE TECHNOLOGY – LIFE CYCLE COSTS

So far, we have seen that technologies are more appropriate when they:

- use local resources
- are community operated
- use renewable energy
- have little effect on the environment
- use energy efficiently.

Life cycle cost must be considered when choosing an appropriate technology. The life cycle cost includes the first cost of the technology as well as the cost over time to use, repair, and replace.

A technology is more appropriate if it is durable and reliable over time. It is durable if it lasts a long time, and it is reliable if it does not need much maintenance or repair.

UNIT VIII: BECOMING A SKILLED TEST TAKER
and
APPROPRIATE TECHNOLOGY IN REVIEW

INTRODUCTION

In almost any subject you study in school, sooner or later you will probably be tested on how well you know the material. Some students don't mind tests or see them as a challenge. Others think they are a bother. Some students are frightened by tests. They feel that no matter how well they know the material, they will not do well on the test.

Good test taking skills can help you do better on tests *and* make you feel more confident about taking them. In this unit you will learn several skills that will help you show what you have learned in science. Some of the skills are general test taking skills. Others will help you with certain kinds of questions, such as multiple choice and true/false questions.

PREPARING FOR A TEST

Studying for a test can be an important part of learning in science. It is your chance to pull together all of the new ideas you have learned. Who knows what other new ideas will become clear to you along the way?

To be a skilled test taker, you need to start reviewing before the day of the exam. Use the tips below to prepare for the test.

1. *Look over your notes and assignments several times before the test.* Once you find out when the test will be, figure out how much time you'll need to study for it. Plan two or three study times during the week before the test. On the last night before an exam, you should be looking over your notes and assignments for the last time, not the first time.

2. *Keep your notes and assignments in chronological order (by date).* You might try putting dividers between units. It is easier to go over material in the same order in which you studied it. This is especially true when the ideas build on one another, as they do in this book.

3. When you go back over a unit's worth of notes for the first time, *underline the main ideas and key words* with a brightly colored marker. Then each time you review that unit, you can zero in on the key words.

4. Some textbooks, like this one, have summaries at the end of each chapter or unit. *Reviewing summaries* is a good way to study for a test.

5. *Study with a friend some of the time, if you can stay mostly on task.* Many people learn effectively when they talk about the subject with another person. So, if you can stay mostly on the task of reviewing, you can gain a lot by studying with a friend some of the time. The rest of the time you'll want to study by yourself. (Of course, if you don't stick to the subject with your friend, "studying" together won't help you at all.)

EXERCISE I

Directions: For homework tonight, begin to prepare for a test on Units I-VII of this book. Follow the steps below.

1) Plan several study times.

2) Organize all of your notes and assignments.

3) Underline main ideas and key words.

4) Read the unit summaries.

TAKING COMMAND OF THE TEST

Once you have reviewed for a test and know the material, you can use other skills to become a better test taker.

When faced with a test, most students tackle the questions in the order in which they are given. Sometimes they are slowed down by difficult questions and never reach questions they could have answered towards the end of the test.

You can avoid this problem by TAKING COMMAND OF THE TEST. To do this, start by quickly reading over the test from beginning to end. Like surveying before you read, this gives you an idea of what to expect.

As you survey the test, fit each question into one of these four categories. This will help you organize how you will answer the questions.

1. *Quick and easy questions* — Questions you know the answer to right away that take little time to answer.

    These will probably be multiple choice, true/false, or short answer questions. Answer these questions as you find them. Answering these questions will help you to build your confidence and may provide you with information that can help you to answer other questions on the test.

2. *Easy but time consuming questions* — Questions to which you know the answer but which will take more time.

    These questions may involve solving a math problem or writing a short essay. Don't stop surveying the test to answer these questions. Instead put a check (√) in the margin next to these questions and go on with the survey. Once you have surveyed the test and answered all of the quick and easy questions, go back and answer the questions you have checked.

3. *Hard questions* — Questions you are not sure you know the answer to or problems you're not sure you can solve.

    When you find these questions as you survey the test, put an "x" in the margin next to them. Work on these questions only after you have answered those in groups 1 and 2.

4. *Impossible questions*

    You may have forgotten to study for these questions, or you may not understand them. Maybe you just can't remember the answer. No matter what the reason, when you find these questions during your survey, put a question mark (?) next to them. Work on these questions only when you have answered all of the other questions.

WARNING: Don't spend too much time dividing up the test questions into these four groups. If you can't make up your mind about a question, put it in the harder of the two groups you are considering and go on. Remember: You only earn points by answering questions, not by grouping them!

If you are not allowed to write on the test, use scrap paper for your survey.

EXERCISE II

Directions: Your teacher will give you a copy of a test on the first seven units of this book (or another test for practice). You will have around 7 minutes to take command of this test by surveying the questions. Remember these steps as you survey.

1) Answer the *quick and easy* questions.

2) Put a check (√) next to questions that are *easy but time consuming*. Then go on.

3) Put an "x" next to questions that are *hard*. Then go on.

4) Put a question mark (?) next to questions that look *impossible*.

MULTIPLE CHOICE AND TRUE/FALSE QUESTIONS

You can do better on a test if you know how to answer different kinds of test questions.

Multiple choice questions ask you to choose the right answer from several possible answers. To answer multiple choice questions:

1. Read the question carefully. Then try to answer the question in your mind *before* you look at the choices.

2. Read all of the choices given and pick the best answer. Sometimes two answers may be right in some way. You need to choose the better one.

3. Be sure to read all of the choices given, even if the first or second one seems right. The best answer may be the last choice. Sometimes the last choice is "all of the above."

4. If you are not sure of the answer, lightly cross out the choices you know are wrong. Then pick the best answer from the remaining choices. If you still aren't sure, make a good guess. If you will lose points for wrong answers, you should guess only if you can cross out all but two answers.

True/false questions ask you to decide whether a statement is true or false. To answer true/false questions:

1. Read the statement carefully. If *any part* of the statement is false, then it is a false statement. Mark it false.

2. Watch for key words such as *always, only, all, never, often*. These words give you clues about whether the statement is true or false.

On most multiple choice and true/false questions, it is worth guessing if you are unsure of an answer. If you will lose points for wrong answers, you should only guess if you can narrow your choices down to two. Don't guess if your teacher tells you not to do so.

EXERCISE III

Directions: Answer the questions on Part I and Part II of the Review Test on Units I-VII (or the questions your teacher gives you for practice). Use the tips for answering multiple choice and true-false questions on page 63.

OTHER TEST-TAKING TIPS

You may find some of these tips helpful as you take a test. Some tips will be more useful than others depending on the test and the situation.

1. *Keep your eye on the clock* — Don't spend more time on a question than it is worth.

2. *Beware of "quicksand questions"* — Don't get stuck on any one question, or you might not have time to finish the test. Go on to other questions, and come back to those that will take a long time. (Surveying the test will help.)

3. *Put your memory on automatic* — Don't waste valuable time trying to remember something on the tip of your tongue. Put your memory on "automatic search," and go on to the next question. If the answer to the first question pops into your mind, go back and answer it.

4. *Read carefully* — Even if you think you know what to do on a question or section of a test, read the directions before beginning work. You never know when the directions may change. One question may ask you to answer in complete sentences. Another may ask for an answer in certain units, such as kilowatt-hours or gallons of oil.

5. *Draw diagrams* — A picture can be worth a thousand words! You can often organize your ideas about a question with a simple picture or diagram. This can make it easier to write the answer later.

EXERCISE IV

Directions: Complete the test on Units I-VII. Use the tips in this unit to be a skillful test taker.

UNIT VIII SUMMARY

Preparing for tests

Part of being a good test taker is preparing in advance for the test.

1. Look over notes and assignments several times.

2. Keep notes and assignments in chronological order (by date).

3. The first time you review, underline main ideas and key words. Each time you review, you can focus on what you have underlined.

4. Review unit summaries.

Taking command of the test

When you get to the test, first survey and categorize the questions.

1. Answer *quick and easy questions* right away.

2. Check (√) *easy but time consuming questions*. Go back to them as soon as you have surveyed the test and answered the quick and easy questions.

3. Put an "x" next to *hard questions*. Answer them after you have done the easier ones.

4. Put a question mark (?) next to *impossible questions*. Try these questions after you have answered all of the others.

Multiple choice and true/false questions

You can be a better test taker if you know how to answer different kinds of questions.

Multiple choice questions: Read the question and try to think of the answer before reading the choices. Read all of the choices, and pick the best answer. If you are not sure of the answer, cross out the choices you think are wrong and choose the best remaining answer.

True/false questions: If the statement is partly false, mark it false. Watch out for key words such as *always, often,* or *never*. These words can help you decide if the statement is true or false.

Other tips for test takers

1. Keep aware of your time.

2. Beware of "quicksand questions." Don't get stuck on one question; go on to the next. You can always come back if there is time.

3. Put your memory on automatic for answers that seem to be on the tip of your tongue.

4. Read directions and questions carefully.

5. Draw diagrams to help organize ideas and answers.

PART TWO:

THE SOLAR GREENHOUSE AS AN APPROPRIATE TECHNOLOGY

UNIT IX: USING SCIENTIFIC MEASURING TOOLS
and
TRAPPING THE SUN'S ENERGY

INTRODUCTION

The solar greenhouse is one example of an appropriate technology.

— It is fairly simple to build and use.

— It uses sunlight, which is a locally available and renewable energy resource.

— It has little, if any, harmful effect on the environment.

In the next four units, you will experiment with some of the ideas that go into making and using a solar greenhouse.

Unit IX will show you how to use two scientific measuring tools — a thermometer and a protractor— that will help you experiment with solar energy.

READING THERMOMETERS

You have probably used a thermometer at home to find out the temperature outside or to see if you had a fever. A thermometer is also a useful scientific tool.

In a thermometer, the liquid inside the glass tube expands when it is heated and contracts or shrinks when it cools. The scale printed on the thermometer helps you "read" the temperature. The position of the liquid on the scale is the temperature of the air, water, or whatever it is you are measuring.

Example: The thermometer below shows a reading of 30° C.

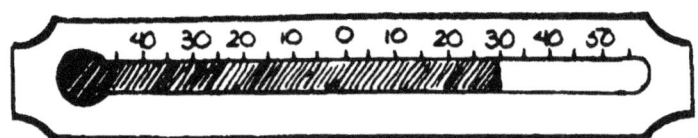

EXERCISE I

Directions: Below are sketches of four thermometers, each showing a different temperature. All of the thermometers use the Celsius scale. With your partner or group, figure out the temperature shown on each thermometer. Write the temperature in the space provided below the thermometer.

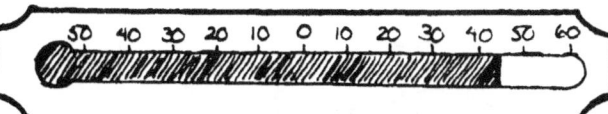

1. _____ 2. _____

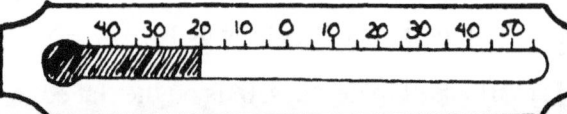 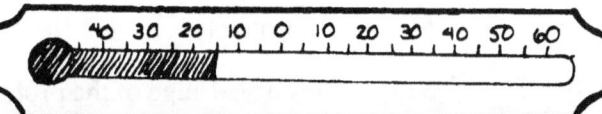

3. _____ 4. _____

PROTRACTORS: MEASURING ANGLES

Sometimes you need to be able to measure the size of an angle in order to do a scientific experiment. Angles are measured in degrees, as in the samples shown below.

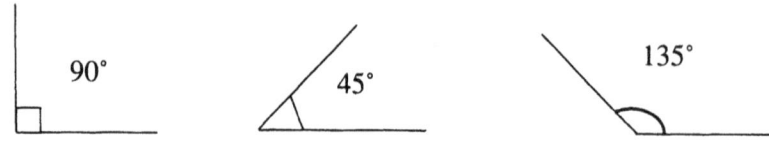

You use a protractor to measure angles. Look at the drawing of the protractor below as you read the explanation of how to use it.

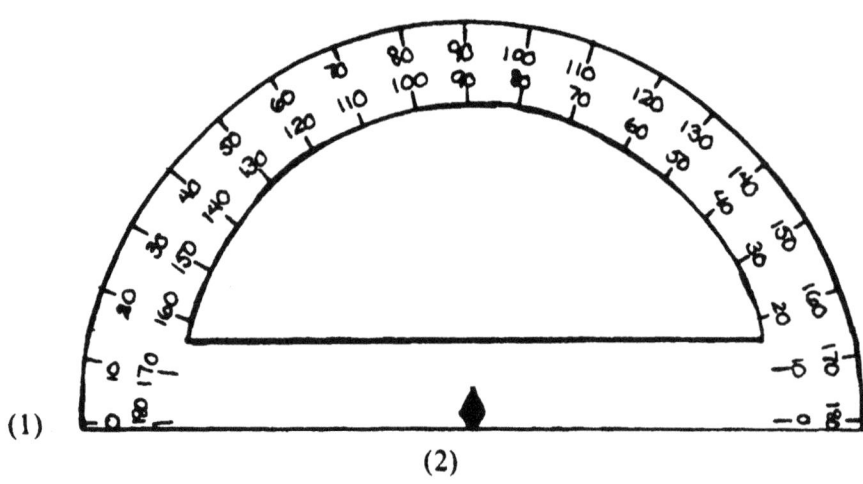

Explanation:
- All protractors have a flat edge (1) with a mark exactly in the center (2).

- The curved edge of the protractor is marked off in degrees. 0° is on the flat edge of the protractor, and 90° is at the top of the curve.

- A protractor may have two scales. The scale that starts with the 0 at the right is used to measure angles that open to the right:

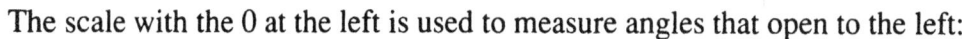

The scale with the 0 at the left is used to measure angles that open to the left:

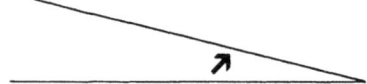

- To measure an angle, place the flat edge of the protractor along one line of the angle. The center mark should be on the point where the two lines meet. Follow the other line of the angle out to where it crosses the scale you are using. The point on the scale where the line crosses is the measure of the angle.

Example: The angle below measures 65°.

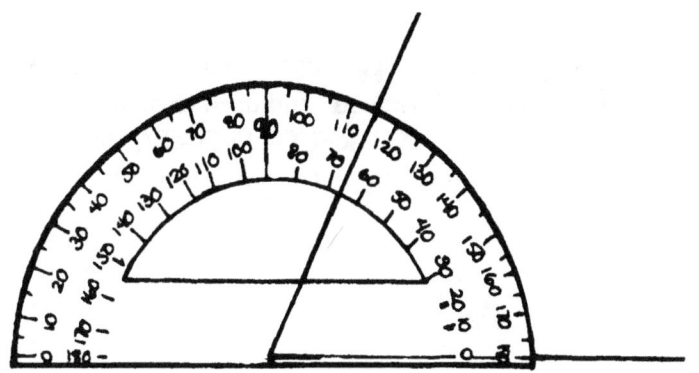

EXERCISE II:

Use a protractor to measure the angles below. Write your answers in the space provided below each angle.

A. _____   B. _____

C. _____   D. _____

EXERCISE III

Directions: In this exercise you and your partner or group will do an experiment that will show you how solar energy can be "trapped" and used to heat air. In this experiment you will A) SET UP, B) GATHER AND RECORD DATA, and C) DRAW CONCLUSIONS. Follow the steps below to carry out this experiment.

A. SETTING UP

1. Gather the following materials:

    2 thermometers
    a protractor
    a notebook
    a dark cardboard divider and a piece of cardboard large enough to shade the notebook
    a large glass jar with a screw-on lid
    a watch or clock
    a pencil
    a light source (you will use sunlight or a lamp provided by your teacher)

2. If your teacher has not yet done so, use a hammer and nail to make a hole in the lid of the jar into which one thermometer fits. To do this, remove the lid from the jar and carefully hammer the nail through it. Make the hole large enough for the thermometer by moving the nail around.

3. If you are using the sun as your light source, take your materials outside and find a level place to set up. If you are using a lamp, clear a space on which to work.

4. Insert the cardboard divider into the jar. Put the lid on, and insert the thermometer through the hole in the jar lid. Tilt the jar and prop it up so that it receives direct light all along one side. Make sure the cardboard is between the light source and the thermometer. The divider will keep the light from hitting the thermometer directly. Use a protractor to measure the angle the bottom of the jar makes with the level surface. Write the angle you have measured here:

    _____

5. Place a notebook on the ground next to the jar. Immediately prop the second piece of cardboard so it completely shades the notebook. Then place the second thermometer on the shaded notebook.

B. GATHERING AND RECORDING DATA

1. Write down the following pieces of information in the spaces provided:

   Temperature outside when you start the experiment: _____

   Temperature in the jar when you start the experiment: _____

2. You are going to check the temperature of the air inside the jar and the temperature of the air outside the jar every 2 minutes for 10 minutes. Use the data table below to write down the temperatures you read every 2 minutes.

TIME	TEMPERATURE IN THE JAR	TEMPERATURE OUTSIDE THE JAR
0 minutes		
2 minutes		
4 minutes		
6 minutes		
8 minutes		
10 minutes		

3. After you have recorded the temperatures for 10 minutes, have your partner stand in the spot where his or her shadow blocks the sun from the jar (or turn off the light). Continue to read the temperatures inside and outside the jar every 2 minutes for the next 10 minutes as you did before, recording your information on the data table continued below.

TIME	TEMPERATURE IN THE JAR	TEMPERATURE OUTSIDE THE JAR
10 minutes		
12 minutes		
14 minutes		
16 minutes		
18 minutes		
20 minutes		

(Continued on page 72)

C. DRAWING CONCLUSIONS

Use the information on your data tables to answer the questions below.

1. Which was hotter after 10 minutes, inside the jar or outside the jar?

   _____

2. Why do you think this happened?

   _____

   _____

   _____

3. What happened to the temperatures when the shadow was on the jar?

   Inside the jar: _____

   _____

   Outside the jar: _____

   _____

4. Why do you think this happened?

   _____

   _____

   _____

THE GREENHOUSE EFFECT

What you have observed in this experiment is the GREENHOUSE EFFECT. When light passes through glass and touches cool surfaces, most of it changes to heat. As heat, it cannot leave the jar as easily as it entered, so the temperature in the jar rises. A solar greenhouse works in the same way that your jar did to trap the sun's energy and change it into heat. The cartoon on page 73 may help you understand the greenhouse effect.

In the experiment in Exercise III, you had to tilt the jar to let in as much sun as possible. Then you measured the angle between the jar and the ground. When you compare this angle to those of your classmates, you will probably find that they are about the same. The best angle for catching the sun depends on how high the sun is above the horizon. If you did this experiment again at another time of day, you would probably choose a different angle to tilt the jar. If you did the experiment during another season of the year, or in a different place on earth, the best angle would again be different.

If you were building a solar greenhouse, you would have to find the best angle for catching the sun. The greenhouse should be positioned so that most of the glass faces south. The glass should be tilted so that it traps as much solar energy as possible during the winter months. You would also have to watch out for trees and buildings that might cast a shadow on the greenhouse during the winter, cutting it off from its energy source.

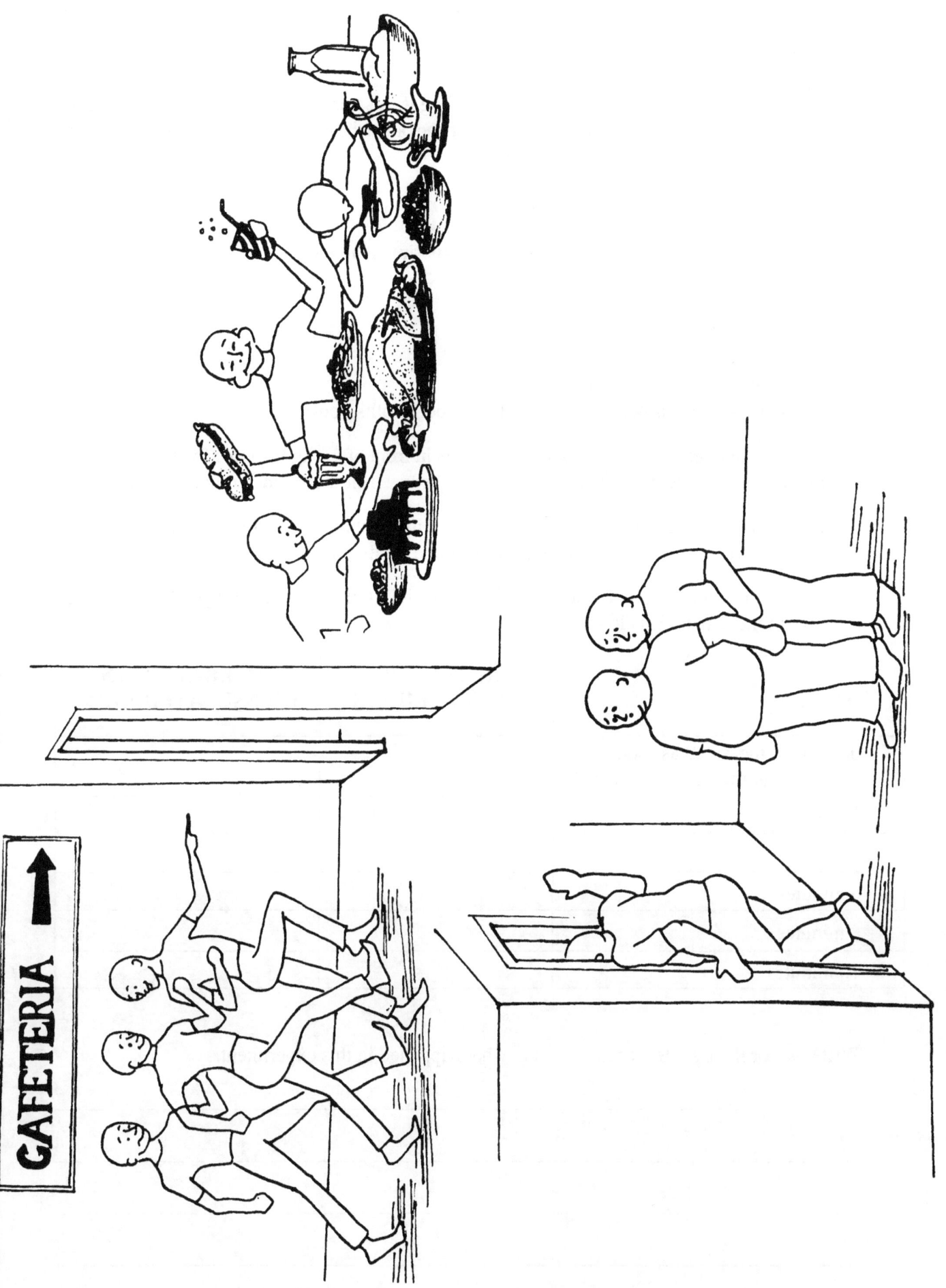

INSULATION

Glass is good at trapping heat but not good at holding it. A solar greenhouse uses INSULATION in the walls and roof to keep the heat in during the winter and out in the summer. Some solar greenhouses also use insulation over the glass on winter nights.

EXERCISE IV

Directions: Follow the steps below to carry out an experiment about insulating a solar greenhouse.

1. You will need these materials:
   - 2 jars with lids (and cardboard dividers)
   - 2 thermometers
   - light source (sun or lamp)
   - some kind of insulation (construction paper, cloth, wool)

2. Put a thermometer into each jar, and place both jars in front of the light source for 10 minutes. Be sure the cardboard dividers are inserted into the jars between the thermometers and the light source.

3. After 10 minutes, immediately wrap one of the jars with whatever insulation you have chosen and remove both jars from the light source (put them in a shady place).

4. Check the temperatures of both jars every 2 minutes for 10 minutes. Record your temperature readings in the data table below.

TIME	TEMPERATURE IN INSULATED JAR	TEMPERATURE IN UNINSULATED JAR
0 minutes (measured as soon as you put the jars in the shade)		
2 minutes		
4 minutes		
6 minutes		
8 minutes		
10 minutes		

5. Write two or three sentences that explain what happened in this experiment.

_____

_____

_____

_____

UNIT IX SUMMARY

MEASURING TOOLS

Measuring tools can help you carry out scientific experiments and answer questions about things you see around you.

In a THERMOMETER, the liquid expands or contracts to show the temperature of air, water, or whatever you are measuring.

You use a PROTRACTOR to measure angles.

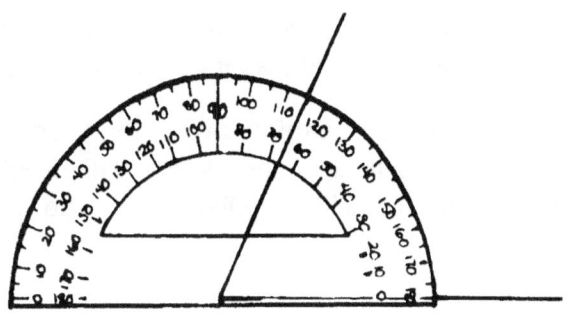

TRAPPING THE SUN: THE SOLAR GREENHOUSE

A solar greenhouse traps the sun's energy and uses it to heat the air inside. This is called the greenhouse effect. A solar greenhouse is most effective when:

1) the greenhouse faces south so that it receives as much sun as possible in the winter,

2) the glass is tilted so that as much sunlight as possible strikes it at a 90° angle for as long each day as possible, and

3) the outside surfaces of the greenhouse are well insulated and tightly built to cut down on heat loss to the outside air.

The solar greenhouse is a good example of appropriate technology. It uses a locally available and renewable source of energy. It also does little to change or hurt the environment. A solar greenhouse uses energy efficiently. It is a technology that is easy to understand and build, and one that helps people be more self sufficient in producing heat and food.

UNIT X: APPLYING SCIENTIFIC LAWS
and
HOW DOES ENERGY BEHAVE
IN A SOLAR GREENHOUSE?

INTRODUCTION: SCIENTIFIC LAWS

Even though you may have a few more years to go before you can get a driver's license, you probably know about the laws that tell drivers what they can and cannot do in a car.

Laws exist in science, too. Scientific laws are people's attempts to explain what happens in nature. Scientific laws cannot be broken. Energy and matter could not disobey them if they tried!

As a science student you can use scientific laws as keys for understanding nature. The more scientific laws you know and understand, the more keys you will have. The trick is knowing which key to use. This unit will help you learn the skill of applying scientific laws to what you see.

EXERCISE I

Directions: Using the skills you have learned in earlier chapters, SURVEY and READ the information on the following pages. Use the space following each section of the reading to MAP or OUTLINE that section. Then you will be able to use the information later in the unit.

As a review of what you have read, do the REVIEW on page 81.

WHAT IS MATTER?

Matter is the "stuff" that everything is made of. It usually occurs as small clumps or bunches called *molecules*. Molecules are too small to see even with a powerful microscope.

Matter exists in three forms: *solid, liquid,* and *gas*.

When a few billion molecules are very close together, they form a *solid*, such as a rock, a tree, or a bird. Solids tend to have a definite shape.

The molecules in a *liquid*, like water, are much farther apart than they are in a solid. In a liquid, the molecules tend to take on the shape of the container that holds them.

The molecules that make up a *gas*, like air, are very far apart. The molecules of a gas tend to spread out to fill a container, like the air molecules in a balloon.

MAP OR OUTLINE:

LAW OF CONDUCTION

The Law of Conduction describes how heat behaves in a solid. This law says that whenever one part of a solid is warmer than another part, heat will travel from the warm part to the cool part, until all parts of the solid are the same temperature. Conduction also explains how heat travels from one material to another when the materials are touching. These materials can be the same or different forms of matter. Heat flows from the warmer material to the cooler.

Conduction occurs whenever one molecule in a solid is warmer than the molecules next to it. The warmer molecule contains more energy, which makes it vibrate faster than the others. Because the molecules in a solid are packed closely together, the warmer, vibrating molecule bumps into its cooler neighbors. This causes them to vibrate faster and become warmer. The first molecule gives up, or conducts, some of its energy when it bumps into its neighbors. This makes it vibrate more slowly and become cooler.

Meanwhile, the other molecules have begun to vibrate faster. Each of these molecules bumps into its neighbors, transferring energy in the form of heat even further away. Conduction stops when all the molecules in a solid are vibrating at the same rate and are therefore the same temperature.

The picture below shows how conduction works.

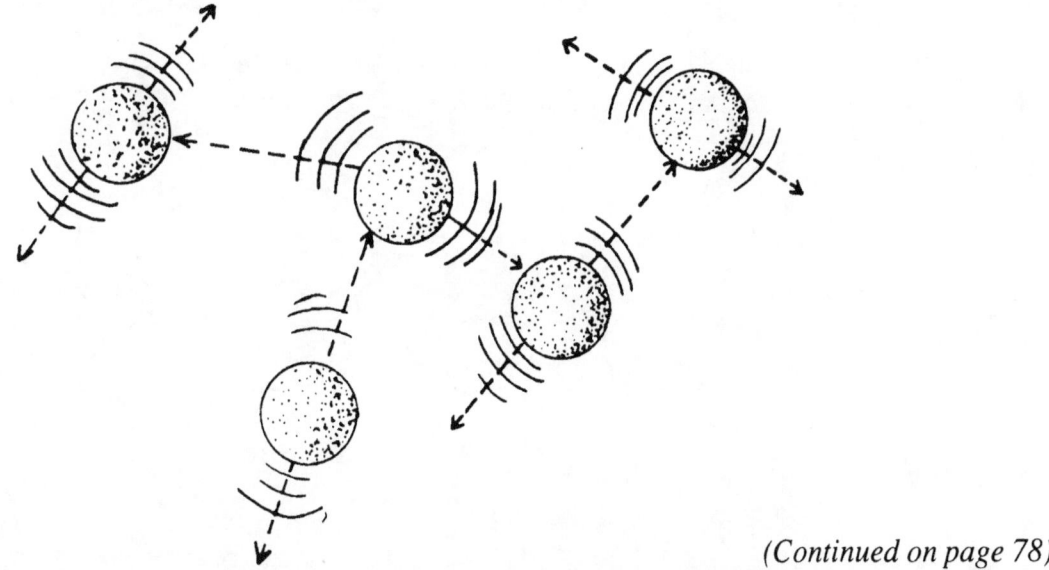

(Continued on page 78)

Some solids conduct heat better than others because their molecules are closer together. Examples of good conductors are metals, concrete, and brick. Other solids are not good conductors because the molecules are farther apart. Examples of poor conductors are fiberglass, foam, and down. Poor conductors are good insulators, because they slow down the movement of heat.

MAP OR OUTLINE:

LAW OF CONVECTION

The Law of Convection explains what happens when a liquid or gas is heated. This law says that when a liquid or gas is heated, it expands and rises. When a liquid or gas is cooled, it shrinks, or contracts, and sinks.

Liquids and gases are both *fluids*. The molecules of which they are made vibrate faster when they are heated, just like the molecules in a solid. But because the molecules in a liquid or gas are less tightly packed than the molecules in a solid, they tranfer heat in a different way.

When the molecules in a fluid (liquid or gas) are heated and begin to vibrate faster, they move farther away from each other. This is what we mean when we say that a liquid or gas *expands* when it is heated. As the liquid or gas molecules spread apart, they rise, so the heat is transferred upward.

The same thing happens in reverse when the molecules in a liquid or gas cool. As they vibrate more and more slowly, they move closer together. We say that the liquid or gas is contracting. As the molecules move closer together, they begin to sink.

MAP OR OUTLINE:

(Continued on page 80)

LAW OF RADIATION

The Law of Radiation says that matter gives off or *radiates* energy all of the time. The warmer matter is, the more energy it radiates. When other matter is hit by this radiating energy, it becomes warmer.

When a material is heated, the molecules on its surface vibrate faster. These molecules then give off energy that travels in straight lines in all directions. When this energy reaches the molecules in another object, it starts these molecules vibrating faster and raises their temperatures.

Radiation is a way of transferring energy from one piece of matter to another without the vibrating molecules touching each other or moving from one place to another. As the picture below shows, you don't have to touch the stove to get warm, because it radiates energy.

MAP OR OUTLINE:

REVIEW: Look back over the notes you have taken. With a partner, choose *one* of the scientific laws explained in the readings. Think of an example from your own experience in which you saw the scientific law operating. Write a few sentences below that describe your example.

LAW: _____

EXAMPLE: _____

_____

_____

_____

_____

_____

RECOGNIZING SCIENTIFIC LAWS

To recognize scientific laws as they operate, you can use the three step process of OBSERVING, RECORDING, and COMPARING described below.

1) OBSERVE what is going on in the situation. Every movement, color, sound, smell, taste, and touch can tell you something.

2) RECORD your observations. You may be able to remember many details, but the best way to remember all of them is to write them down. Sometimes there may not be enough time to record everything.

3) COMPARE your observations to other situations in which you saw similar things happening. What law was operating in those situations? Decide which scientific law best explains what you observed and recorded.

EXAMPLES OF THE LAW OF CONDUCTION

You have experienced the law of conduction many times. Perhaps you have had one of these experiences:

1. You leave a cool spoon in a bowl of hot soup. When you pick up the spoon, it has become very hot. Heat has been transferred from the soup to the spoon and up the handle according to the law of conduction.

2. You lean your arm on the desk for a long period of time. When you lift it up, you find that the place where your arm has been is warm. Heat has been conducted from your arm to the desk top.

Exercises II and III on the next page will show you examples of the laws of convection and radiation.

EXERCISE II

Directions: Your teacher will demonstrate another scientific law for you. Follow the steps below to see if you can recognize what it is.

1. OBSERVE what the teacher does.

2. Use this space to RECORD what you see happening:

3. COMPARE this to other situations that seemed similar.

4. Which scientific law does this experiment show? _____
_____

EXERCISE III

Directions: Follow the steps below to see a third scientific law at work.

SET UP

1. You will need: a light bulb (plugged in)
   a piece of cardboard

OBSERVE AND RECORD

2. Plug in the light bulb. Hold your hand to one side of the bulb without touching it.

   What happens to the temperature of your hand? _____

   _____

3. Leave your hand to one side of the light bulb. Hold the cardboard between your hand and the bulb.

   What happens to the temperature of your hand? _____

   _____

COMPARE

4. Can you think of other situations in which you experienced something similar? What laws were in action in those situations? Discuss this with your group.

5. What scientific law does this experiment show? _____

   _____

83

SCIENTIFIC LAWS AND THE SOLAR GREENHOUSE

The solar greenhouse operates according to the scientific laws of conduction, convection, and radiation. Remember:

One example of *conduction is* the transfer of heat through solid matter.

Convection is the transfer of heat in a liquid or gas. Heated fluids expand and rise. Cooled fluids contract and sink.

Radiation is the transfer of energy from the surface of an object into space.

The arrows in the solar greenhouse below show where conduction is occurring. Read the explanation as you look at the picture.

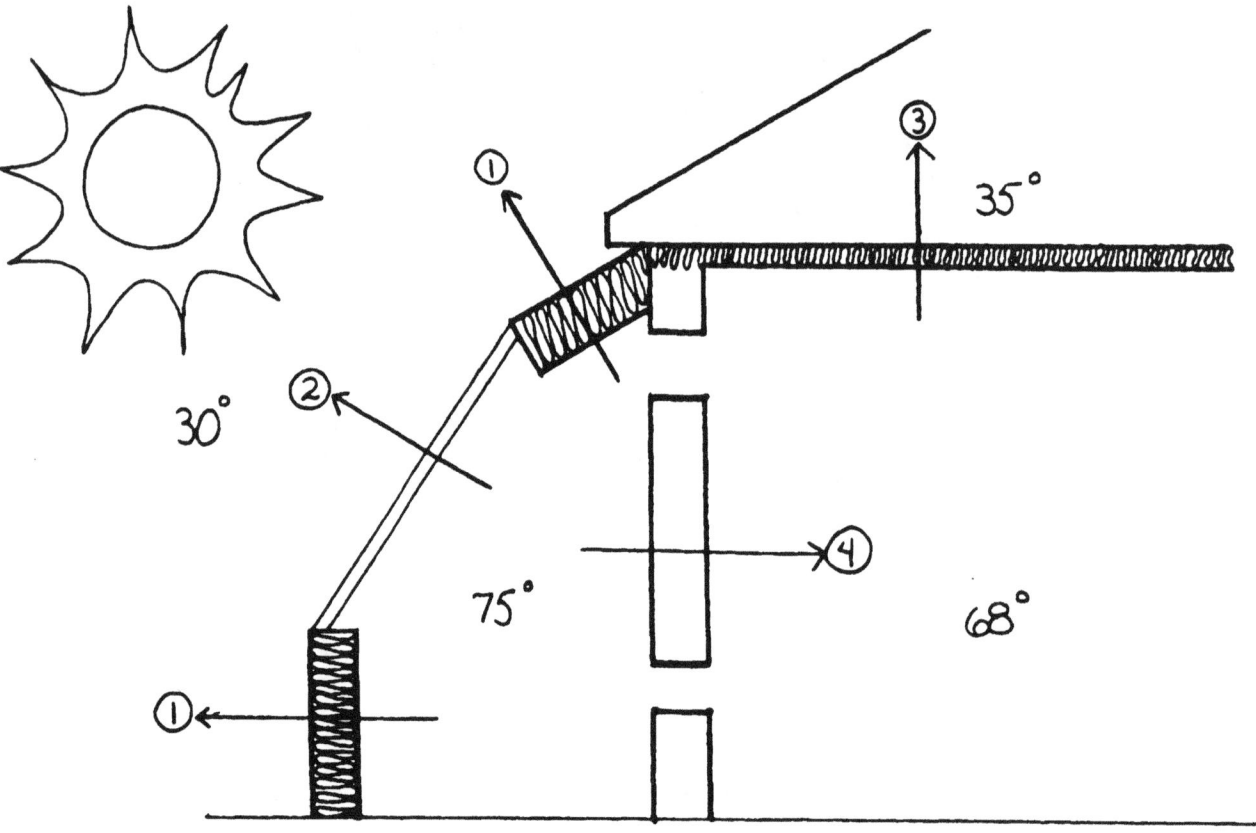

Explanation:
- Heat is conducted through walls and roof to the outside (arrows #1). If walls contain materials that are poor conductors (insulation), heat will be lost more slowly.

- Heat is conducted through the glass to the outside (arrow #2). If there are two layers of glass with an air space between them, heat will be lost more slowly.

- Heat is conducted through the ceiling to the attic (arrow #3). Again, insulation here would slow down heat loss.

- Heat is conducted through the wall to the house, helping to heat the house (arrow #4).

EXERCISE IV

Directions: The pictures below and on the next page show the same solar greenhouse as on page 84. Each picture has arrows that show a scientific law of heat transfer in action. For each picture:

 1) Observe — look carefully to see what is happening.

 2) Record what is happening at each arrow in the space provided.

 3) Compare what you have recorded to the examples of scientific laws in Exercises II and III.

 4) Explain which scientific law is shown by the arrows.

Picture 1

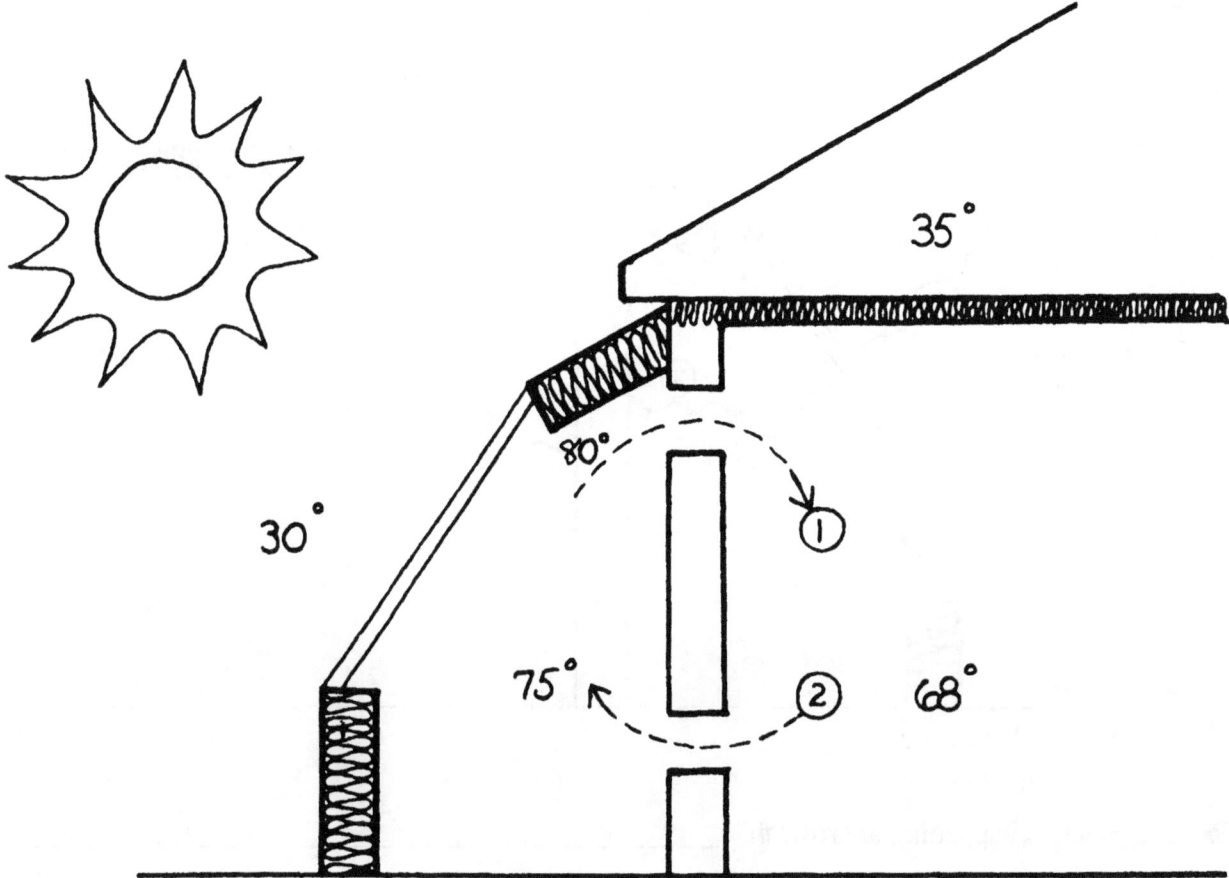

1. Observe what is happening.

2. Record: What is happening at arrow #1? _____

   _____

   What is happening at arrow #2?

85

3. Which example from Exercises II and III is similar to what you see happening with these arrows?
   _____

   How are they alike? _____
   _____

4. Which scientific law do these arrows show? _____
   _____

Picture 2

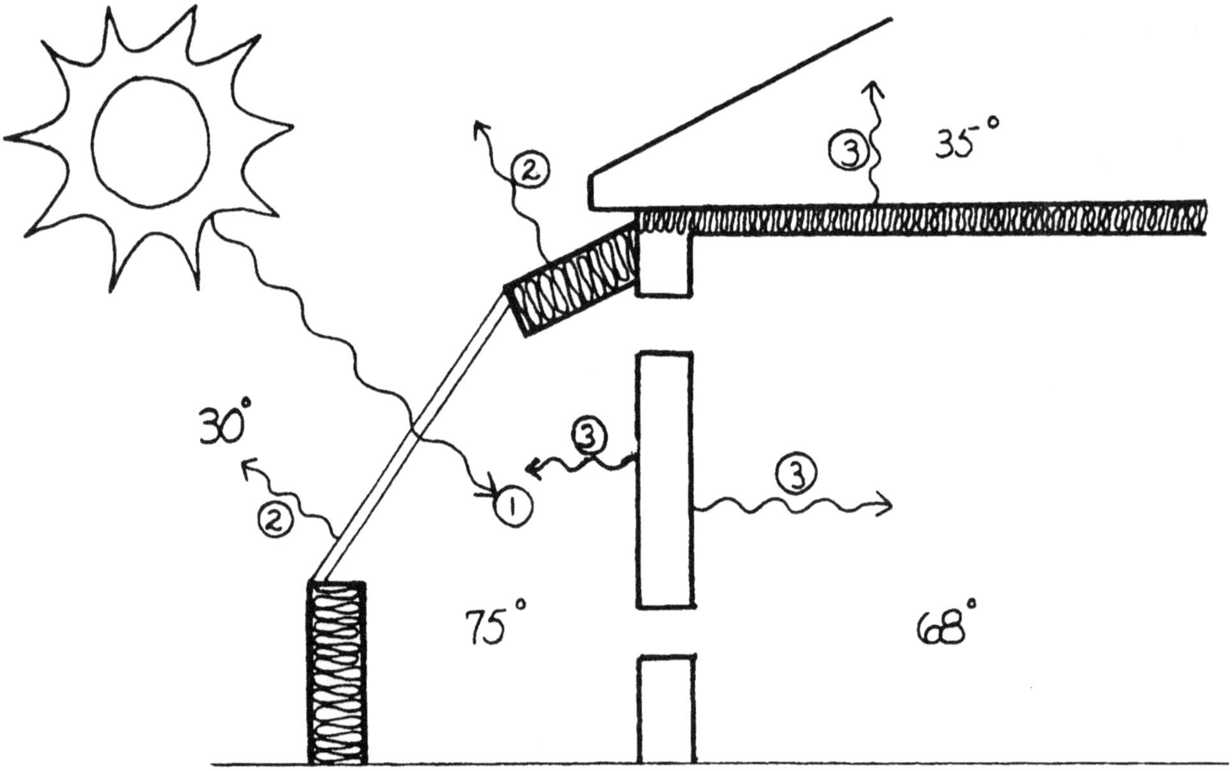

1. Observe what is happening.

2. Record: What is happening at arrow #1? _____
   _____

   What is happening at the arrows marked #2? _____
   _____

   What is happening at the arrows marked #3? _____
   _____

3. Compare: Which example from Exercises II and III is similar to what you see happening in this picture? _____

_____

How are they alike? _____

_____

4. Which scientific law do the arrows in this picture show? _____

_____

UNIT X SUMMARY

APPLYING SCIENTIFIC LAWS:

To figure out which scientific law is operating in a situation, follow these steps:

OBSERVE what is happening.

RECORD all of your observations.

COMPARE what you see to other situations in which you know what law is operating. Then decide which scientific law explains your observations.

SCIENTIFIC LAWS AND THE SOLAR GREENHOUSE

Scientific laws describe how matter and energy behave.

Matter is the "stuff" everything is made of. It exists in very small bunches, called *molecules*.

When the molecules are close together, the matter forms a *solid*.

When the molecules are farther apart, the matter is a *liquid*.

When the molecules are very far apart, the matter is a *gas*.

Three scientific laws of heat transfer operate in a solar greenhouse.

The *Law of Conduction:*	Whenever one part of a solid is warmer than another part, heat travels from the warm part to cooler parts until the solid is all the same temperature. Through conduction, heat escapes through the solid surfaces of a solar greenhouse. To slow down this heat loss, you must use materials that are poor conductors to insulate walls and ceilings.
The *Law of Convection:*	When a liquid or gas is heated, it expands and rises. When it cools, it contracts and sinks. Warm air from a solar greenhouse rises by convection and moves into the attached building. Cool air from the building moves back into the greenhouse to be reheated.
The *Law of Radiation:*	Matter radiates energy in straight lines. Warm matter radiates more energy than cool matter. When matter is struck by radiant energy, it becomes warmer. A solar greenhouse receives radiant energy from the sun. At the same time, the outside surfaces of the greenhouse radiate heat back into space. Heat also radiates from the back wall of the greenhouse into the adjoining building, providing a source of heat for the building.

UNIT XI: WORKING WITH THE METRIC SYSTEM
and
HOW CAN WE STORE ENERGY?

INTRODUCTION: THE METRIC SYSTEM

In the United States, we are used to measuring distance in inches and feet and weighing things in ounces and pounds. This is known as the English system of measuring.

In science, you will find measurements in another system, the METRIC SYSTEM. The metric system is used in almost all other countries. This unit will help you learn to "think metric" and use the metric system as a scientific tool.

MEASUREMENTS IN THE METRIC SYSTEM

You may already use some metric measurements without knowing it. For example, temperatures measured in degrees Celsius are metric, while those in degrees Fahrenheit are English. Below are three other units of measurement in the metric system.

> The **METER** is a unit of length, like a foot or yard. A meter is about three feet long.
>
> The **LITER** is a unit of volume, like a quart or gallon. A liter is about the size of a quart.
>
> The **GRAM** is a unit of mass or the quantity of matter. Anywhere on earth an object's mass is the same as its weight. One thousand grams is approximately two pounds.

In the English system, we change from inches to feet to yards to show a longer length. In the metric system, a prefix before the unit tells you the number of meters, liters, or grams being measured.

> **KILO** – means 1,000. A kilometer is 1,000 meters. A kilogram is 1,000 grams.
>
> **CENTI** – means 1/100. A centimeter is 1/100 of a meter. A centigram is 1/100 of a gram. Or, 100 centigrams = 1 gram.
>
> **MILLI** – means 1/1,000. A millimeter is 1/1,000 of a meter. A milligram is 1/1,000 of a gram. Or, 1,000 millimeters = 1 meter. 1,000 milligrams = 1 gram.

EXERCISE I

Directions: Use the information you have just learned about the metric system to answer the questions below and on the next page.

1. It is three kilometers from one town to the next. How many meters is it? _____

_____

2. A meter stick is 1 meter long. How many centimeters are there on the meter stick? _____

_____

3. A container of water weighs 4,000 grams. How many kilograms does it weigh? _____

_____

4. A feather weighs 1 milligram. How many grams does it weigh? _____

STORING SOLAR ENERGY

The solar energy entering a solar greenhouse turns into heat when it strikes the floor, the walls, and even the plants. On a sunny day, the greenhouse can quickly get too warm. There are several ways to prevent overheating. The most common one is to store the extra energy for use at night or on cloudy days.

There are many ways to store energy. A car battery stores electrical energy produced by the running engine. A watch spring stores energy when you wind it. A dam stores energy when it holds back water that can be released to generate electricity. Non-renewable energy is already stored in the form of coal, oil, and natural gas.

For a solar greenhouse to store energy, it must contain materials that can soak up heat like a sponge. Materials used in this way are called *thermal mass*. An ideal material for storing energy in a solar greenhouse would hold large amounts of heat and take up a small space. It would also be a material that loses heat slowly.

In Exercises II and III you will experiment with several different materials to see which would be most appropriate for use as thermal mass in a solar greenhouse.

EXERCISE II

Directions: Follow the steps below to carry out an experiment about how different materials store heat.

SET UP

1. You will need these materials:

    3 identical glass jars with screw-on lids (one hole in each lid)
    3 Celsius thermometers
    an energy source (sun or heat lamp)
    material to put in jars, such as sand, rock, air, water, wood chips, clay

2. Weigh the empty jars. Use a scale that measures in grams. Write the weight of each jar in the appropriate space below.

    _____   _____   _____
              Jar 1   Jar 2   Jar 3

3. Fill each jar with a different material. Weigh each jar. Record these weights in the appropriate spaces below. Then subtract the weight of jar 1 when empty from the weight of the same jar when filled. The difference is the weight of the material in the jar. Write this number in the appropriate space. Then do the same for jars 2 and 3.

	Material	Weight of filled jar	Weight of empty jar	Weight of material in jar
Jar 1				
Jar 2				
Jar 3				

4. Screw on the jar lids, and insert a thermometer through the hole in each lid. Place all three jars at an equal distance from the light source. Be sure that none of the jars is shaded and that all have the same amount of surface facing the light source.

OBSERVE AND RECORD

5. Record the beginning temperature of each jar in Data Table #1 on the next page. Then measure the temperature in each jar at 2 minute intervals, recording your information in Data Table #1. Continue measuring the temperatures until all the temperatures seem to stop rising.

(Continued on page 92)

Data Table #1

	Jar 1 Material:_____	Jar 2 Material:_____	Jar 3 Material:_____
Beginning temp.			
2 minutes			
4 minutes			
6 minutes			
8 minutes			
10 minutes			
12 minutes			

6. Remove the jars from the energy source. Measure the temperatures at 2 minute intervals for 10 minutes. Record your data in Data Table #2 below.

Data Table #2

	Jar 1 Material:_____	Jar 2 Material:_____	Jar 3 Material:_____
Beginning temp.			
2 minutes			
4 minutes			
6 minutes			
8 minute			
10 minutes			

EXPLAIN

7. Using the information from Data Tables #1 and #2, answer these questions:

   a) Which material reached the highest temperature? _____

   b) Which material stayed the coolest? _____

   c) Which material dropped the fewest number of degrees after you removed the jars from the energy source? _____

   d) Which material dropped the greatest number of degrees after you removed the jars from the energy source? _____

COMPARE

8. If other groups in your class used different materials, compare your results to theirs. Look for:

   Which material got hottest?

   Which material stayed the coolest?

   Which material had the greatest temperature drop in the given time?

   Which material had the least temperature drop?

MEASURING HEAT: JOULES

It is possible to measure the amount of heat a material absorbs, or takes in and holds.

The unit of heat in the metric system is the JOULE.

It takes about 4.17 JOULES of heat to raise the temperature of 1 gram of water 1 degree Celsius. If 1 gram of water starts at 10 degrees Celsius and is heated to 11 degrees Celsius, it has absorbed 4.17 Joules of heat. If it is heated to 15 degrees Celsius, it has absorbed 20.85 Joules of heat.

To find out how many Joules of heat a material has absorbed, multiply its weight in grams by the change in temperature by 4.17. In the example above, 1 gram of water x 5° Celsius x 4.17 = 20.85 Joules.

Example: If 100 grams of water is heated and its temperature is raised 20° Celsius, how many Joules have been added?

  100 grams of water x 20° Celsius x 4.17 = 8,340 Joules

Remember: Heat, measured in Joules, and temperature, measured in degrees, are not the same. Heat depends on the amount of material. Temperature does not. A teaspoonful of water and a bathtub full of water may both be at the same temperature: 30° Celsius. But the bathtub contains more heat, or Joules, and will therefore cool more slowly.

EXERCISE III

Directions: Use the information you recorded in Exercise II to fill in the blanks below. First write the name of each material you used in the spaces provided. Then for each material, write the information asked for. This information will help you find out how much heat each material absorbed.

MATERIAL 1: _____

1. What was the weight of this material? _____ grams

2. What was the beginning temperature? _____ ° Celsius

3. What was the highest temperature this material reached? _____° Celsius

4. What was the change in temperature? (Subtract the beginning temperature from the highest temperature.) _____ ° Celsius

5. Find how many Joules the material absorbed. Multiply the weight in grams by the change in temperature by 4.17.

    Write your result here: _____ grams x _____ ° Celsius X 4.17 = _____ Joules

MATERIAL 2: _____

1. What was the weight of the material? _____ grams

2. What was the beginning temperature? _____ ° Celsius

3. What was the highest temperature this material reached? _____ ° Celsius

4. What was the change in temperature (highest temperature minus beginning temperature)? _____ ° Celsius

5. How many Joules did this material absorb? (Multiply grams x change in temperature x 4.17)
    _____ grams x _____ ° Celsius x 4.17 = _____ Joules

MATERIAL 3: _____

1. What was the weight of the material? _____ grams

2. What was the beginning temperature? _____ ° Celsius

3. What was the highest temperature this material reached? _____ ° Celsius

4. What was the change in temperature (highest temperature minus beginning temperature)? _____ ° Celsius

5. How many Joules did this material absorb?
    _____ grams x _____ ° Celsius x 4.17 = _____ Joules

Now answer these questions:

1. Which material was exposed to the most heat? _____
   _____

2. Which material absorbed the most heat (the greatest number of Joules)? _____
   _____

3. Which material would you choose to store heat in a solar greenhouse? _____
   _____

   Why? _____
   _____
   _____

UNIT XI SUMMARY

WORKING WITH THE METRIC SYSTEM

The metric system is a way of measuring distance, volume, weight, temperature, and heat. In the metric system:

A **meter** is a unit of length.

A **liter** is a unit of volume.

A **gram** is a unit of mass or weight.

Temperature is measured in **degrees Celsius.**

A **Joule** is a unit of heat. It takes about 4.17 Joules to raise the temperature of 1 gram of water 1° Celsius.

In the metric system, prefixes are added to show the number of each unit being measured.

Kilo = 1,000. A kilometer = 1,000 meters.

Centi = 1/100. A centimeter = 1/100 meter. 100 centimeters = 1 meter.

Milli = 1/1,000. A millimeter = 1/1,000 meter. 1,000 millimeters = 1 meter.

STORING ENERGY IN A SOLAR GREENHOUSE

Energy can be stored for use at a later time. Non-renewable energy is already stored in the form of oil, gas, and coal.

A solar greenhouse will overheat on a sunny winter day unless something is done with the extra heat. One solution is to store the extra heat for use at night or on a cloudy day.

Materials that absorb and store heat are called *thermal mass*. Air is not an appropriate thermal mass because it cannot store very much heat without becoming too hot for a solar greenhouse. Water is a very appropriate thermal mass because it can store a lot of heat at a low temperature. It also cools very slowly.

UNIT XII: WORKING WITH LARGE NUMBERS
and
HOW CAN WE CONSERVE ENERGY?

INTRODUCTION

Heat escapes from many different places in a house or building. Look at the sketch below. Draw arrows to show where you think heat escapes from this house or is wasted in this house. Then label each arrow. One arrow has been drawn and labeled as an example.

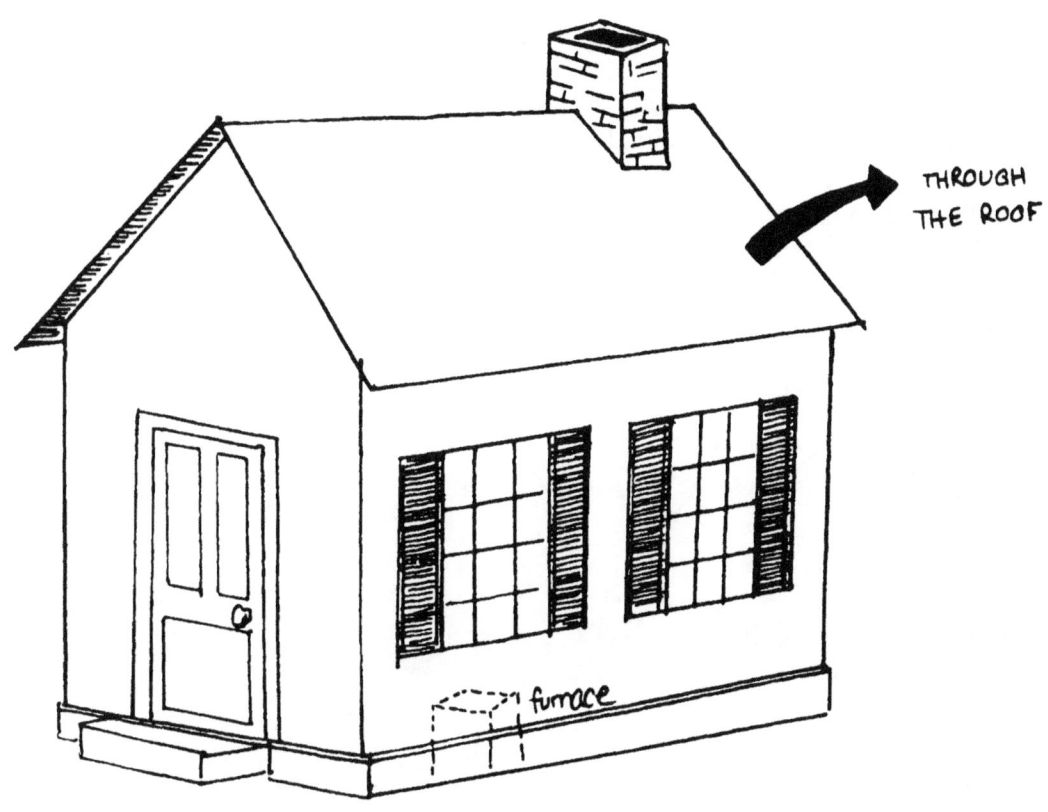

CONSERVING ENERGY

So far you have learned about trapping and storing solar energy in a solar greenhouse. But trapping and storing energy is of little use if the energy is allowed to escape into the outside air. We also need ways of keeping energy from being lost or wasted. This is called *conserving energy*. This unit will show you several ways of conserving energy in a house or building:

WORKING WITH LARGE NUMBERS

To understand the amount of heat that enters and leaves a building, you need to be able to work with very large numbers. These numbers are too big for most hand calculators. Fortunately, scientists have developed a system of dealing with large numbers. This system is called SCIENTIFIC NOTATION.

In SCIENTIFIC NOTATION, the number 1,000,000,000,000.0 is written as 1.0×10^{12}

- Notice that in scientific notation the decimal point is moved so there is only one digit to the left of the decimal point, in this case a 1. *The number of places the decimal point has been moved is shown by the number above and to the right of the 10.* This number is called the *exponent*. In 1×10^{12} the exponent is 12. This means the decimal has been moved 12 places to the left.

- The number with the decimal point is called the *coefficient*.

Look at the examples below.

a. $1,000,000,000,000 = 1.0 \times 10^{12}$ (coefficient, exponent)

b. $150 = 1.5 \times 10^{2}$ (coefficient, exponent)

c. $1,850,000 = 1.85 \times 10^{6}$ (coefficient, exponent)

EXERCISE I

Directions: In Part A, put each number into scientific notation.
In Part B, write out the number that is shown in scientific notation.

PART A   **Scientific Notation**

1. 1,000   1. _____

2. 3,250,000   2. _____

3. 43,000   3. _____

PART B   **Number Written Out**

4. 6×10^{5} 4. _____

5. 1.2×10^{2} 5. _____

6. 7.32×10^{3} 6. _____

WORKING IN SCIENTIFIC NOTATION

Numbers written in scientific notation can be added, subtracted, multiplied, and divided.

Adding and Subtracting

To add or subtract numbers in scientific notation, you must be sure that the *exponents* are the same.

You can add 4×10^3 and 3×10^3, but you cannot add 4×10^3 and 3×10^2.

If you have to add 4×10^3 and 3×10^2, you can change one of them so the exponents are the same. For example, you could say:

$$4 \times 10^3 = 4{,}000 = 40 \times 10^2$$

Then you could add 40×10^2 and 3×10^2

Once the exponents are the same:

TO ADD: *Add the coefficients.*

$$(40 \times 10^2) + (3 \times 10^2) = (40 + 3) \times 10^2 = 43 \times 10^2 = 4.3 \times 10^3$$

TO SUBTRACT: *Subtract the coefficients.*

$$(40 \times 10^2) - (3 \times 10^2) = (40 - 3) \times 10^2 = 37 \times 10^2 = 3.7 \times 10^3$$

Multiplying and Dividing

When you multiply or divide in scientific notation, the exponents do not have to be the same.

TO MULTIPLY: *Multiply the coefficients and add the exponents.*

$$(6 \times 10^2) \times (4 \times 10^3) =$$

$$(6 \times 4) \times (10^{2+3}) = 24 \times 10^5 - 2.4 \times 10^6$$

↑ Multiply coefficients   ↑ Add exponents

TO DIVIDE: *Divide the coefficients and subtract the exponents.*

$$(6 \times 10^4) \div (3 \times 10^3) =$$

$$(6 \div 3) \times (10^{4-3}) = 2 \times 10^1 = 20$$

↑ Divide coefficients   ↑ Subtract exponents

EXERCISE II

Directions: Do the problems below to practice adding, subtracting, multiplying, and dividing in scientific notation. Use the examples on page 99 for help.

1. $(6 \times 10^3) + (5 \times 10^3) = $ _____

2. $(9 \times 10^4) - (8 \times 10^6) = $ _____

3. $(2 \times 10^2) \times (6 \times 10^4) = $ _____

4. $(8 \times 10^8) \div (4 \times 10^3) = $ _____

5. $(4 \times 10^4) + (3.2 \times 10^4) = $ _____

6. $(5.6 \times 10^5) - (3 \times 10^5) = $ _____

7. $(3 \times 10^5) \times (9 \times 10^3) = $ _____

8. $(9 \times 10^7) \div (3 \times 10^4) = $ _____

HEATING YOUR HOME

Scientific notation can be helpful in figuring out how to keep heat in your house in the winter.

Heat is measured in British Thermal Units, or BTUs. A BTU is the amount of heat needed to raise the temperature of one pound of water one degree Fahrenheit. A gallon of fuel oil contains about 140,000 BTUs (1.4×10^5) of heat.

In the northern part of the U.S., a three bedroom house might use 1,000 (1×10^3) gallons of fuel oil each winter. To find out how many BTUs of heat this house would use, you would multiply the number of BTUs contained in one gallon of fuel oil by the total number of gallons of fuel oil used.

$$(1.4 \times 10^5) \times (1 \times 10^3) = 1.4 \times 10^8 \text{ BTUs}$$

↑   ↑

BTUs from   Total
1 gallon of   gallons of
fuel oil   fuel oil used

This sample house uses 1.4×10^8 BTUs each winter. If you can find out how much fuel oil *your* home uses every winter, you can use the same formula to find how many BTUs you use. If your home is heated by electricity or natural gas, you can use a similar formula. One kilowatt hour contains 3,414 BTUs. One hundred cubic feet of natural gas contains 103,000 BTUs.

CONSERVING HEAT

Anything that can be done to keep heat from leaving the house saves energy and money. One way to conserve energy is to be sure that your furnace works efficiently. Other ways are:

1) insulating your house;

2) putting up storm windows to slow down the loss of heat from windows;

3) closing drapes every night and opening them in the morning; and

4) turning down the thermostat when people are out or asleep.

EXERCISE III

Directions: Work through the steps of the problem on the next page to find out how many gallons of oil can be saved by insulating the attic of a house. Use scientific notation to help you work with the large numbers.

Background Information

Houses A and B both have 1,000 square feet of floor area in the attic. House A's attic is insulated. House B's attic is not.

House A loses $.66 \times 10^3$ BTUs every hour through the ceiling.

House B loses 3.6×10^3 BTUs every hour through the ceiling.

1. The heating season for these houses consists of 3,000 (3×10^3) hours.

    a) How many BTUs will House A lose through its insulated ceiling during a heating season?

    $.66 \times 10^3$ BTU/hour × 3×10^3 hours = _____
    ↑ BTUs lost each hour   ↑ Number of hours per heating season   ↑ BTUs lost in heating season

    b) How many BTUs will House B lose through its uninsulated ceiling during a heating season?

    3.6×10^3 BTU/hour × 3×10^3 hours = _____

2. How many BTUs does House A save by being insulated? Find the difference between the total number of BTUs lost in House B and House A.

    _____ − _____ = _____
    ↑ BTUs used in House B   ↑ BTUs used in House A   ↑ BTUs saved

3. Find out how many gallons of oil are saved by insulating House A. Divide the number of BTUs saved by the number of BTUs in one gallon of oil (1.4×10^5).

    _____ ÷ 1.4×10^5 BTU/gallon = _____
    ↑ BTUs saved   ↑ BTUs in 1 gallon   ↑ Gallons saved

THE COST OF SAVING ENERGY

Two of the four suggestions given on page 101 for saving energy cost no extra money. *Closing the drapes* and *turning down the thermostat* save energy and money but cost you nothing.

It does cost money to add *storm windows* or *insulation* to your house. You can find out how much it costs and compare it to how much you save. It may take several months or years to *pay back* the cost of the insulation or storm windows out of the money they save you. But once this amount of time has passed, the savings and the conservation of energy continue.

By investing money in your house to save energy, you can often save more money on heating bills than you could have earned by putting the same amount of money in the bank. You have also helped to conserve a finite source of energy.

UNIT XII SUMMARY

SCIENTIFIC NOTATION

Scientific notation is a system for working with large numbers. In scientific notation, the number 1,000,000,000 is written as: 1.0×10^9.

The 1 is the *coefficient*.

The 9 is the *exponent*. It shows how many places the decimal point has been moved to the left.

Numbers in scientific notation can be added, subtracted, multiplied, and divided.

To ADD or SUBTRACT, the exponents must be the same.

TO ADD: Add the coefficients. Keep the exponent the same.

$$(3 \times 10^2) + (6 \times 10^2) = 9 \times 10^2$$

TO SUBTRACT: Subtract the coefficients. Keep the exponent the same.

$$(8 \times 10^4) - (4 \times 10^4) = 4 \times 10^4$$

You can multiply or divide in scientific notation even if the exponents are different.

TO MULTIPLY: Multiply the coefficients and add the exponents.

$$(2 \times 10^4) \times (6 \times 10^2) = 12 \times 10^6$$

TO DIVIDE: Divide the coefficients and subtract the exponents.

$$(9 \times 10^6) \div (3 \times 10^4) = 3 \times 10^2$$

CONSERVING ENERGY

It is not enough to trap and store solar energy for later use. We must also find ways to slow down the loss of heat from a house or building. Otherwise, much of the heat collected by the greenhouse will be wasted. Slowing down the rate of heat loss is a method of *conserving energy*.

There are many ways to conserve heat:

1) Be sure that your furnace is working efficiently.

2) Insulate the attic.

3) Put up storm windows that keep air from escaping from windows.

4) Close the drapes each night and re-open them every morning.

5) Turn down the thermostat when people are out or asleep.

All of these forms of conservation will save energy and money. The first three ways of conserving energy listed above will also cost money. It may take several months or years to *pay back* the cost of conserving out of the savings. But once the payback time has passed, the conservation and savings continue.

PART THREE:

APPROPRIATE TECHNOLOGY AT WORK

UNIT XIII: DEVELOPING AND TESTING AN HYPOTHESIS and APPLYING APPROPRIATE TECHNOLOGY

INTRODUCTION

This unit will give you a chance to try out many of the ideas you have learned about appropriate technology by creating a device to trap and use renewable energy. By comparing your device to those created by your classmates, you should be able to come up with some changes that will improve its performance.

PASSIVE SOLAR COLLECTORS AND WIND MACHINES

In Exercise I on page 106 you will build either a passive solar collector or a wind machine. Both of these devices are explained below and on the next page. The explanations describe the purpose of both devices, how you will test their performance, and what materials you can use to build them.

Passive Solar Collector

Purpose: To raise the air temperature to a comfortable level and maintain that temperature for as long as possible.

Test: You will test this device by letting it collect solar energy until the air inside reaches a temperature of 21°C. You will then remove it from the light source and measure how long it takes before the temperature falls to 15°C.

Part	Commercial Material	Your Material	Purpose
Transparent cover	glass, plexiglass	plastic wrap	allows light to enter, traps heat
Structure to be heated	house, greenhouse	shoe box, coffee can, jar, wood box	uses heat
Storage material	slate, rock, dark-colored tiles, water	dark stones, gravel, dark sand, water	stores heat and returns it to space gradually
Insulation	fiberglass, cellulose, styrofoam	any insulating material	keeps heat from leaving space too quickly

PASSIVE SOLAR COLLECTOR

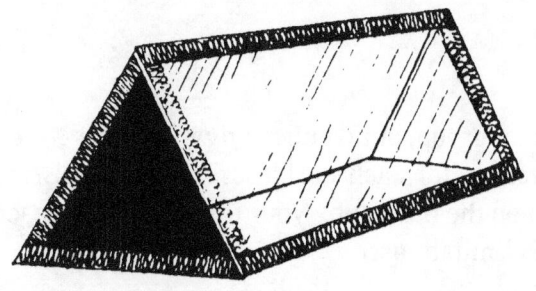

Wind Machine

Purpose: To make an axle turn as quickly as possible, generating energy for other uses.

Test: You will test this device by painting one blade a bright color. You will then count how many times the blade goes around in a three minute period when exposed to a wind source.

Part	Commercial Material	Your Material	Purpose
Blade(s)	light metal, wood, cloth	cardboard, balsa wood, metal, plastic, cloth	catches wind energy
Axle (may be horizontal or vertical)	metal	metal, wood, plastic	turns as blades turn, producing electrical or mechanical energy
Support tower	metal	wood, metal	supports axle and blade and raises them into wind current

WIND MACHINE

EXERCISE I

Directions: With your partner or group, build either a *passive solar collector* or a *wind machine*. The purpose and materials for each are described above. Bring your device to class. Be prepared to test it on the day set by your teacher. (Your teacher will tell you if there are size and materials limitations.)

SCIENTIFIC METHOD

Once you have built your passive solar collector or wind machine, you must test its ability to perform the task for which it was designed. No matter how well it works, there will probably be changes you can make in its design that will improve its performance.

When engineers or scientists wish to improve the performance of a technology, they usually use the scientific method.

1. They OBSERVE the technology or device in operation.

2. They FORM AN HYPOTHESIS about why the device performed as it did and what they could do to make it perform better.

3. They TEST THEIR HYPOTHESIS by changing their device and observing it in operation once again.

4. They DRAW A CONCLUSION about the truth of their hypothesis.

In the rest of this unit, you will have a chance to use the scientific method to improve the performance of the device you built.

EXERCISE II

Directions: Try out your device, using one of the tests described below. Then compare your device to those tested by other groups. List all of the differences you can observe between the devices that worked well in the test and those that did not.

I. Test for Passive Solar Collector

1. Insert a thermometer into your passive solar collector.

2. Place the solar collector in the sun (or next to a reflector lamp). Leave it there until the thermometer measures 21 °C.

3. Remove the solar collector from the light source. Time how long it takes for the temperature in the solar collector to drop to 15° C.

   Record the time here: _____

II. Test for Wind Machine

1. Paint one blade a bright color.

2. Place your wind machine outside in the wind (or in front of a fan.)

3. Count how many times the colored blade goes around in a three minute period.

   Record the number here: _____

III. Compare your results to those of other groups

If you built a solar collector, list all of the differences you see between collectors that worked well and those that did not.

If you built a wind machine, list all of the differences between those that worked well and those that did not.

Kind of device you built: _____

Differences: _____

_____

_____

_____

_____

_____

DEVELOPING AN HYPOTHESIS

An HYPOTHESIS is an idea about why something happens the way it does. It is usually based on information that has been gathered or observed. An hypothesis is a good guess based on facts; it is not a sure thing until it has been tested and proven.

You have just gathered information about how different passive solar collectors and/or wind machines work. You can now develop an hypothesis from this information that explains what makes a passive solar collector or wind machine work most effectively. For example, one hypothesis might be:

A passive solar collector will work better if it is insulated.

EXERCISE III

Directions: Look again at the list of differences you found between devices (Exercise II, above). As a group, write three hypotheses about what makes the kind of device you built (either passive solar collector or wind machine) work most effectively.

Hypothesis 1: _____

_____

_____

Hypothesis 2: _____

_____

_____

Hypothesis 3: _____

_____

_____

TESTING HYPOTHESES

Once you have developed an hypothesis, you must test it to determine whether or not it is true. You can do this by changing your device in the way suggested by your hypothesis. Then you can re-test your device to see if it is actually more effective. If it is, the hypothesis is correct. If it is not, the hypothesis is probably incorrect.

To be tested, your hypothesis should involve only one idea or part of your device. Then you will know which one thing to change before you re-test your device and will have only one reason for any difference in its performance. For example, if your hypothesis is:

A good passive solar collector has insulation and dark-colored storage materials,

you would not know whether the change in the insulation or the change in the storage materials caused a change in performance when you re-tested your device. A better hypothesis would be:

A good passive solar collector is well insulated.

You could then change the kind or amount of insulation in your passive solar collector to test this hypothesis.

EXERCISE IV

Directions: Follow the steps below to test your hypothesis.

I. Look over the hypotheses you wrote in Exercise III (page 108). Choose one or rewrite one that you can test. Be sure that it involves changing only one thing about your device. Write the hypothesis you will test here:

_____

_____

_____

II. Change your device (improve it!) in a way that allows you to test your hypothesis.

III. Use the same test you used in Exercise II (page 107) to re-test your improved device. Remember that the conditions of the test must be the same, so that the only change is the one you made to the device. Record your results in the space provided below.

Passive solar collector: Time for temperature to fall from 21°C to 15°C:

_____

Wind machine: Number of times the blade goes around in three minutes:

_____

IV. Compare the results of your first test in Exercise II and this re-test.

Was the performance of your device improved? _____

Was your hypothesis correct? _____

DRAWING A CONCLUSION

After you have observed something happening and developed and tested an hypothesis about it, you are ready to draw a *conclusion*. A conclusion is a statement that says whether or not your hypothesis is true.

For example, suppose your *hypothesis* was:

A good passive solar collector needs insulation.

If, when you added insulation to your device, you found that it was more effective at trapping and holding heat, your *conclusion* would be:

A good passive solar collector needs insulation.

If your testing proved that insulation did not result in improved performance, your *conclusion* would be:

Insulation does not improve a passive solar collector.

EXERCISE V

Directions: Write a conclusion that explains whether the hypothesis you tested in Exercise IV was true or false. Write your conclusion on the lines provided below.

CONCLUSION: _____

_____

_____

_____

UNIT XIII SUMMARY

DEVELOPING AND TESTING AN HYPOTHESIS

An hypothesis is a careful guess about why something happens. It is based on observed facts.

You can use the SCIENTIFIC METHOD to develop and test an hypothesis.

1. OBSERVE to collect information.

2. DEVELOP AN HYPOTHESIS that explains your observations.

3. TEST YOUR HYPOTHESIS through some kind of experiment, and observe your results.

4. DRAW A CONCLUSION that states whether your hypothesis was true or false.

APPROPRIATE TECHNOLOGY

Passive solar collectors and wind machines are examples of appropriate technology at work. In this unit you have seen how changes can be made to improve the performance of these technologies.

UNIT XIV: PUTTING IT ALL TOGETHER

INTRODUCTION

This book has introduced you to information and ideas about appropriate technology. In this unit you will have the chance to use your knowledge in a real situation. With a group of your classmates, you will identify a problem in your school that could be solved using appropriate technology. You and your classmates will then work to solve the problem, using the science learning skills and ideas you have learned in this book.

Some examples of problems worked on by other groups of students include:

1) litter;
2) wasted energy;
3) wasted food;
4) garbage disposal, recycling, and composting; and
5) transportation.

EXERCISE I

Directions: With your group, identify four problems in your school that could be solved using appropriate technology. You may want to use the list of problems above for ideas, but the problems you identify should be more specific to your situation. Write the problems on the lines provided below.

Example: In our school, lights are left on in empty classrooms so that energy is wasted.

Problems:

1. _____
   _____

2. _____
   _____

3. _____
   _____

4. _____
   _____

SOLVING THE PROBLEM

Once you have identified a problem, you have to plan a strategy for solving it. Remember how Lisa solved her problem in Unit VII?

The paragraphs below describe several examples of strategies used by students to help their communities solve problems through the use of appropriate technology. Your local problems may be different from those presented here. You may also have less time to solve your problem than some of these groups did. But perhaps their ideas will be useful to you in organizing your own problem solving project.

Examples of Local Problem Solving

1. In San Jose, California, a group of 20 third, fourth, and fifth graders formed an Energy Patrol to help their school save electricity. Each day, four Energy Patrol members pick up special jackets, name tags, and keys kept for their use in the office. During morning recess, they checked unoccupied areas to see that lights had been turned off. If the lights were on, patrol members turned them off and attached a picture of their school mascot crying about energy waste. If the lights were off, they attached a picture of the mascot smiling. The Energy Patrol saved their school thousands of kilowatt hours of electricity in each of the first three months of their project.

2. A group of Sheehan High School ninth graders in Wallingford, Connecticut were concerned about the energy being wasted in their school. They formed a group called the Wallingford Auditing Technical Team (WATT) to look at the ways their school could save energy. WATT presented its findings to the school board and convinced the board that tremendous amounts of energy could be saved through simple conservation measures like the ones you learned about in Unit XI. The board appointed WATT as its Energy Management Team. In the next two years, the school spent about $12,000 on conservation and saved over $500,000.

3. 250 youths in La Crescenta, California helped to build Sunfire, a 5-kilowatt solar collector. These students designed many parts of the collector, obtained scrap material, and did most of the construction. They planned to donate the collector to Pitcairn Island in the South Pacific. The island suffers from a severe energy shortage.

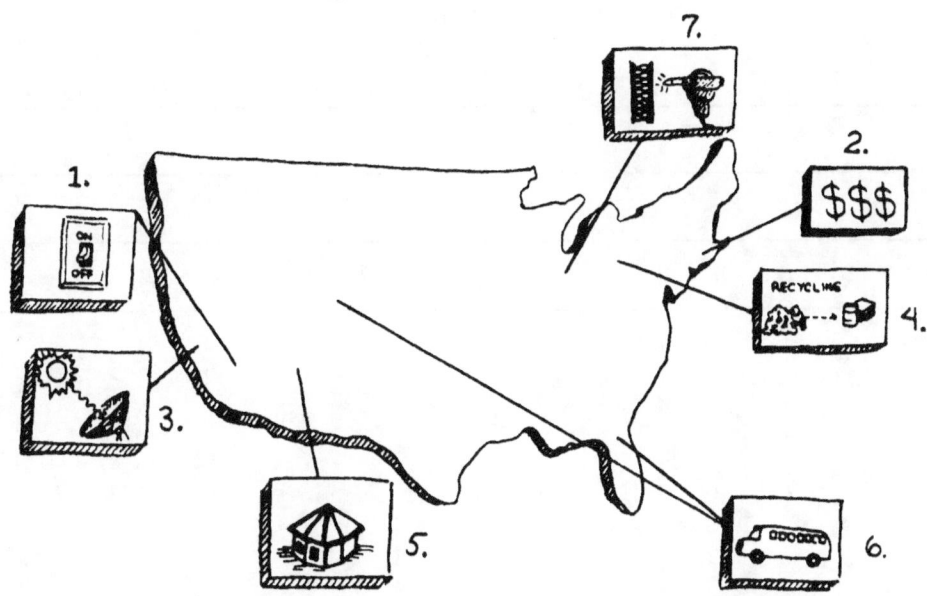

4. Riverside High School students in Ellwood, Pennsylvania were the moving force behind an appropriate technology designed to conserve their community's energy and material resources. These students recycled over 2 million pounds of glass, over 1 million pounds of tin, nearly 3 million pounds of newsprint, and about 1,000 used car batteries. As a result of their recycling efforts, Riverside students contributed close to $6,000 toward school and community projects.

5. Navajo youth in Window Rock School District #8, Fort Defiance, Arizona demonstrated how appropriate technology could help cut their community's dependence on nonrenewable energy by using a plentiful local resource, sunlight. Many of the students had been thinking of dropping out of school before the project began. Instead, they pitched in to design and build a solar hogan, an eight-sided structure that combines traditional Navajo building with modern solar technology. The hogan stirred much interest throughout the Navajo community.

6. Students in two different parts of the United States came up with very different appropriate technologies for solving transportation problems in their communities. These students were concerned about air pollution, traffic problems, and the inefficient use of energy. In Jacksonville, Florida, high school students formed Students for Mass Transit to educate citizens about the need for more public transportation. Students at George Washington High School in Denver, Colorado found another appropriate solution to a similar problem. They organized and operated a computer carpooling service that was used by many Denver businesses and state agencies.

7. Twelve teenagers in Ava, Illinois were trained to identify energy-wasting problems and how to correct them using no cost/low cost weatherization techniques. This group was a part of the Jackson County Action to Save Energy. In only 10 weeks, these students weatherized 50 homes belonging to elderly and low-income members of their community.

EXERCISE II

Directions: With your group, choose one of the problems you or your classmates have identified that you think you can help to solve. Write the problem in the space provided below.

Then write down the information, materials, and steps you will need to take to solve the problem. Use the space provided on the next page.

PROBLEM: _____

_____

_____

_____

(Use your own paper if you need more space for any of these sections.)

Information needed to solve the problem:

Information	Where will you get it?
1. _____	_____
2. _____	_____
3. _____	_____
4. _____	_____
5. _____	_____
6. _____	_____

Materials needed to solve the problem:

Materials	Where will you get it?
1. _____	_____
2. _____	_____
3. _____	_____
4. _____	_____
5. _____	_____
6. _____	_____

Steps you will take to solve the problem:

Step	Who will do it?	By what date?
1. _____	_____	_____
_____		
_____		
2. _____	_____	_____
_____		
_____		
3. _____	_____	_____
_____		
_____		

	Step	Who will do it?	By what date?
4.			
5.			
6.			
7.			

EXERCISE III

Directions: With your group, carry out your problem solving strategy. Your teacher will tell you when during the project you need to report your progress, and when the project should be completed. Present your completed project to the class in one of the ways described below.

Project presentations:

1. A written report describing your project, how you carried it out, and what your results were.

2. A feature article for the local newspaper in which you describe your project and your results. (Read some feature stories from the paper to get an idea of the way this might be written.)

3. An oral presentation to the class that explains the problem, your planned solution, and your results. Charts and pictures will help you in this presentation.

4. A video-taped presentation or video-taped "news show" or "documentary."

5. A picture-presentation (for example, a bulletin board) that describes your problem, how you went about solving it, and your results. This presentation could include writing, drawings, photographs, charts, and whatever else helps to explain your project.

6. A computer-based presentation using Hypercard, Linkway, or a similar program.

UNIT XIV SUMMARY

In this unit you have used many of the science study skills and ideas you have learned to help solve a school problem. By doing this you have shown that appropriate technology is useful in solving local problems. You have also shown that *you* can be an important part of your community's and country's energy and technology future!

GLOSSARY

Acidity – The percentage of acid in something. An acid turns blue litmus paper red. Acids taste sharp and sour. Some acids may burn the skin.

Acre – A unit of area equal to 43,560 square feet.

Active solar – A technology that uses the sun's rays to produce heat and then uses electrically powered fans or pumps to move the heat where it is needed or stored for later use.

Air tight – Closed so tightly that no air or other gases can get in or out.

Anthracite – A kind of coal that is hard and makes little smoke when it burns.

Appropriate – Carefully chosen to fit the situation or use. Suitable, proper.

Atmosphere – The gas that surrounds a body in space, especially around the earth.

Back-up heating – System designed to provide heat when the main system cannot supply enough.

Barrel (of oil) – Equal to 42 gallons and to 5.6×10^6 BTU.

Billion – 1,000,000,000 or 10^9.

Biomass – Any plant material that can be turned into energy.

BTU – British Thermal Unit. One BTU can raise the temperature of one pound of water one degree Fahrenheit.

Carbon dioxide – CO_2. A gas given off by fossil fuels when they burn in an atmosphere containing enough oxygen.

Carbon monoxide – CO. A poisonous gas given off by a fuel burning in an atmosphere containing little oxygen.

Centi- – A prefix meaning 1/100. There are 100 centimeters in a meter. One centimeter = 1/100 or .01 meter.

Climate – The average weather for a region; rainfall, temperature, winds.

Coefficient – In scientific notation, the number multiplied by the 10. In 3×10^6, 3 is the coefficient.

Commercial sector – The part of the economy consisting of offices, schools, retail stores, hospitals, nursing homes, etc.

Community – A group of people living in the same area who act together in some way.

Compost – Partially decomposed organic waste (such as leaves, food scraps, lawn clippings, animal manure) used to enrich soil.

Conduction – The transfer of heat energy from molecule to molecule within a solid. Also the transfer of heat energy from one material to another which touches it.

Conserve – Not waste, make last as long as possible.

Contract – Shrink, occupy a smaller space.

Convection – Transfer of heat energy in gases or liquids. As convection occurs, warmer matter rises and cooler matter sinks.

Converted – Changed from one form to another.

Cord (of wood) – A unit of measure for cut firewood. A cord of wood is equal to a stack that is four feet high, four feet wide, and eight feet long.

Corrode – To wear away or be worn away, especially by chemical action.

Crisis – A time of danger or difficulty in which great changes can take place.

Cubic foot – A unit of volume which is one foot by one foot by one foot.

Deposit – A pool or vein of material like oil or coal which has formed beneath the surface of the earth.

Disposal – The act of throwing away or getting rid of something.

Domestic – At home; within the country.

Efficiency – Getting good results without wasting time, materials, or effort.

Electric resistance heating – Electricity flowing through a wire heats up the wire, which can be used to cook food or heat space or water.

Energy – Ability to move objects or do other kinds of physical work.

English system – A measurement system based on various common forms (foot, yard) which have now been standardized.

Entropy – A measure of the amount of energy unavailable for work, or lost through conversion.

Environment – Surroundings in which a plant or animal lives, including the air, water, and soil.

Expand – Enlarge; occupy a larger space.

Exponent – In scientific notation, the number above and to the right of the 10, indicating the number of times the decimal has been moved. It also indicates how many times 10 is to be multiplied by itself. In 3×10^6, 6 is the exponent.

Finite – Having a definite end, able to be completely used up.

First cost – The amount of money it takes to buy something.

Fluid – Matter that is able to flow; liquids and gases are fluids.

Fluorescent – A type of lighting in which gas molecules are put into motion by electric current; as a result the lamp glows.

Fossil fuel – A burnable material formed over a period of millions of years from decaying plants and animals; oil, coal, and natural gas.

Friction – A force that slows down or stops the motion of two objects as they rub against each other.

Fuel – A material such as wood, coal, gas or oil that is burned to produce energy.

Gas – Matter in which the molecules are far apart and move so rapidly they tend to escape from an open container.

Gram – Basic unit of mass or weight in the metric system. 1,000 grams are equal to approximately 2.2 pounds in the English system.

Greenhouse effect – Heating that results when light passes through a window or other translucent material, changes to heat energy, and cannot escape as quickly as it entered.

GNP – Gross National Product. The total dollar value of all the goods and services produced in a country in a year.

Hydropower – A technology for using the energy contained in falling water to produce electricity or to perform mechanical work.

Inappropriate – Not suitable or proper for a particular situation or use.

Incandescent – A type of lighting in which a thin wire (filament) glows when electricity passes through it.

Industrial sector – The part of the economy involved in the manufacture of products and the mining of fuels and other ores.

Insulated – Surrounded with a material that slows or stops the passage of heat.

Insulation – Any material that does not conduct heat easily. Used to slow down heat loss from a house or building.

Kilo- – A prefix meaning 1,000. A kilogram = 1,000 grams; a kilowatt = 1,000 watts.

Kilowatt-hour – One thousand watts used for one hour. Ten one hundred watt light bulbs left on for an hour would use one kilowatt-hour of electricity.

Kinetic energy – Energy that has to do with motion.

Life cycle cost – The money it takes to buy, use, maintain, and eventually replace something over the entire time it is owned.

Liquid – Matter in which the molecules move more quickly than in a solid. Liquid matter takes on the shape of its container.

Liquified natural gas – To transport natural gas long distances, gas is cooled until it becomes a liquid, because it takes up less space.

Liter – Basic unit of volume in the metric system. One liter is approximately equal to one quart in the English system.

Local – Nearby.

Maintain – Keep in good working order.

Marine – Of or living in the sea.

Matter – Anything which has mass and takes up space.

Mechanical – Having to do with machines or tools.

Meter – The basic unit of length in the metric system. One meter is approximately equal to one yard in the English system.

Methane – A burnable gas which is one part of natural gas and which can also be produced from decaying organic waste.

Metric system – A system of measurement based on tens or powers of ten. In the metric system, 100 centimeters = 1 meter; 1,000 meters = 1 kilometer.

Milled – Ground up into fine pieces.

Milli- – A prefix meaning 1/1,000. A millimeter = 1/1,000 or .0001 meters.

Molecule – Two or more atoms joined by chemical bonds. A molecule is the smallest piece of matter that still has the properties of that form of matter.

Natural gas – A fossil fuel often found with petroleum.

Network – An organization which helps its members share information, goods or services with one another.

Nitrogen – An element that makes up 78% of the atmosphere.

Non-renewable – Consumed faster than it can be replaced.

Nuclear fission – The splitting of certain heavy atoms into lighter atoms. This causes the release of energy.

OPEC – Organization of Petroleum Exporting Countries.

Organic – Of or coming from living things.

Organization – A group of people who come together because they have a common interest or want to accomplish a certain task.

Passive solar – A technology that uses sunlight to heat air and water without the use of electrical fans or pumps.

Payback (or simple payback) – The time needed to save enough money to recover the cost of an investment. (Does not consider the impact of inflation.)

Petroleum – A liquid fossil fuel.

Photon – A particle of light.

Photovoltaics – A technology that turns sunlight into electricity.

Pollution – The process of making air, water, food, etc. harmful to living things; the result of this process.

Protractor – A tool used to measure angles.

Proven reserve – The portion of a coal, oil, or natural gas deposit that can be sold for more than it presently costs to get it out of the ground and prepare it for sale.

Quad – A unit of energy equal to one quadrillion BTUs.

Radiate – Send out in straight lines in all directions.

Radiation – Transfer of energy through space in all directions. Radiation can occur even in a vacuum.

Radon – A radioactive gas produced by the element radium.

Recycle – Turn into something else so that it can be used again.

Reliable – Dependable, trustworthy.

Renew – To make new or like new again; to replace.

Renewable – Capable of being renewed. A renewable resource is replaced almost as quickly as it is used.

Residential sector – The part of the economy which is made of the places in which people live, such as houses, apartments, mobile homes, condominiums, cooperatives.

Resource – A supply of something that is available for use.

Return on investment – Dollars saved divided by dollars invested. Usually expressed as percent.

Revitalized – Put new life into, brought back to life.

Rural - Having to do with the country as opposed to the city.

Scarce – Hard to find, often because there is not much left.

Scientific notation – A system for writing large numbers as single digit numbers times ten to some power. For example, $3,600,000 = 3.6 \times 10^6$.

Shortage – Lack of enough to satisfy a need or demand.

Short ton – A unit of weight equal to 2,000 pounds.

Silicon – The second most common element found in nature, used to make photovoltaic cells.

Solar – Coming from or having to do with the sun.

Solid – Matter in which the molecules are so close together that it retains its shape.

Sprouted – Started to grow.

Standard of living – Measure of what a person spends to support his or her life; the level of comfort in everyday life.

Strip mining – Mining in an open pit after removing the earth and rock covering the deposit.

Sulfur oxides – Chemical compounds containing sulfur and water. When these combine with water, they produce acids that may cause damage to buildings and may be harmful to people.

Sulfuric acid – Acid that results when certain sulfur oxides and water combine.

Technology – Materials, machines, and methods that people use to meet their needs.

Thermal mass – Material that absorbs and stores heat.

Thermometer – A tool used to measure temperature. As the liquid in the thermometer absorbs heat, it expands. As it loses heat, it contracts.

Transportation sector – The part of the economy involved in the movement of goods and people from place to place. Includes cars, buses, trains, planes, ships, pipelines, etc.

Transported – Carried from one place to another.

Trillion – 1,000,000,000,000 or 10^{12}.

Ultimately recoverable resource – A resource that can be put to use at some future time, once it becomes profitable to mine and process it.

Uranium – A heavy element that is naturally radioactive.

Urban – Having to do with the city as opposed to the country.

Vulnerable – Unprotected from danger.

Waste – Something which is thrown away.

www.ingramcontent.com/pod-product-compliance
Lightning Source LLC
Chambersburg PA
CBHW081203240426
43669CB00039B/2798